Aligning Organizational Subcultures for Competitive Advantage

*New Perspectives in Organizational Learning,
Performance, and Change*

Jerry W. Gilley, Series Editor

Aligning Organizational Subcultures for Competitive Advantage

A Strategic Change Approach

Willie E. Hopkins
California State University, Chico

Shirley A. Hopkins
California State University, Chico

Paul Mallette
Colorado State University

BASIC
BOOKS
A Member of the Perseus Books Group
New York

Copyright © 2005 by Willie E. Hopkins
Published by Basic Books
A Member of the Perseus Books Group

Basic Books are available at special discounts for bulk purchases in the United States by corporations, institutions, and other organizations. For more information, please contact the Special Markets Department at the Perseus Books Group, 11 Cambridge Center, Cambridge MA 02142; or call (617) 252-5298 or (800) 255-1514; or e-mail special.markets@perseusbooks.com.

A CIP catalog record for this book is available from the Library of Congress.

ISBN-13 978-0-465-03093-4
ISBN 0-465-03093-9

05 06 07 / 10 9 8 7 6 5 4 3 2

Publisher's Note

Organizations are living systems, in a constant state of dynamic evolution. *New Perspectives in Organizational Learning, Performance, and Change* is designed to showcase the most current theory and practice in human resource and organizational development, exploring all aspects of the field—from performance management to adult learning to corporate culture. Integrating cutting-edge research and innovative management practice, this library of titles will serve as an essential resource for human resource professionals, educators, students, and managers in all types of organizations.

The series editorial board includes leading academics and practitioners whose insights are shaping the theory and application of human resource development and organizational design.

Contents

Acknowledgments

Several individuals participated in the completion of this book, and we would like to acknowledge them. First, we thank Jerry Gilley for encouraging us to submit the proposal that resulted in this book. Next, we thank David Shoemaker and Perseus Books for bringing our ideas to market. We also thank Whitney Miller for her tireless efforts in making copies of articles and helping us with our research for the book, and Dale Maginnis for doing a great job with some of the original graphics used in the book. Finally, we thank the group of anonymous individuals who reviewed the manuscript and whose feedback helped us to sharpen our ideas for the book.

Preface

The Business Management section of commercial bookstores or libraries is likely to be stocked with several books about corporate culture. As you flip through the pages of these books, you will find that corporate culture is generally defined as the predominant value system for the organization as a whole. However, you are not likely to find that large organizations are usually made up of several subgroups of employees who share a value system that may not conform to the predominant value system that defines an organization's corporate culture. In other words, these organizational subgroups possess distinct cultures that are subcultures of an organization's distinctive corporate culture.

Although corporate culture provides the overarching framework for this book, our primary focus is not on this macro-topic but on the micro-topic of organizational subcultures. Specifically, we ask and answer questions such as, What types of subcultures exist in organizations? Which types of subcultures should be of most concern to managers? How might these subcultures be aligned? Why do they need to be aligned? What benefits might be gained from such alignments?

In addition to logical deductions, our research for this book leads us to conclude that organizations whose subcultures are in alignment are more likely to have stronger corporate cultures than those organizations whose subcultures are misaligned. Results of our research also suggest that a strong corporate culture can be a source of competitive advantage (for example, distinctive competence that allows an organization to consistently outperform its competitors), and a competitive advantage in the market-place is associated with high levels of organizational performance.

Management literature contains both descriptive and prescriptive studies related to corporate culture. However, for the practicing manager, this literature is deficient in at least three areas: (1) most of it is in the form of articles, published in a variety of academic and professional journals; (2) virtually all focus on culture within organizations primarily at the macro level; and (3) virtually none focus exclusively on reasons or methodologies for aligning organizational subcultures.

Our purpose in this book is to address these deficiencies by focusing on a topic that should be of vital concern to practicing managers, a topic that existing literature has largely neglected. Such a focus provides an element of newness and convenience by bringing together (in one volume) current and classic research with direct applications to the task of aligning organizational subcultures. Our focus also provides a wealth of practical advice for managers, consultants, and others who seek a clear, workable understanding of this important topic.

We accomplish several tasks in the introductory chapter of this book. First, we encourage the reader to consider the sources of competitive advantage for organizations and whether these sources are effective in a highly competitive global business environment. Second, we set forth corporate culture as an indirect but important source of competitive advantage that is largely overlooked within organizations. Third, we look at the role that subcultures can play in strengthening or weakening corporate culture and, ultimately, organizational performance. Fourth, we provide arguments of why it is imperative that subcultures be aligned with the dominant corporate culture. Fifth, we identify the types of organizations that must be most concerned with subculture alignment. Sixth, we identify the types of individuals within these organizational types who are most likely to assume the responsibility of bringing about this alignment. Seventh, we introduce the strategic change approach to aligning organizational subcultures. Eighth, we provide a preview of background chapters that explain the rationale behind the strategic change approach. Once you have finished reading the introductory chapter, we are confident that you will want to know more about this approach and its potential for helping organizations to gain and sustain a competitive advantage in today's marketplace.

Introduction

Sources of Competitive Advantage

During the 1980s Michael Porter popularized the concept of generic competitive strategies.[1] These strategies include *cost-leadership* (producing goods or services at a cost lower than competitors), *differentiation* (creating a product or service that is perceived by customers to be unique in some important way), and *focus* (concentrating on serving a particular market niche). These competitive strategies are called generic because any organization can adopt them—whether its focus is manufacturing or service, whether for-profit or not-for-profit—to gain a competitive advantage. Indeed, domestic companies such as Dell Computers, H. J. Heinz, Schlitz Brewing, National Can Company, and Brooks Brothers have adopted these generic strategies, as have international companies such as BMW (Germany), Seiko (Japan), Bang & Olufsen (Denmark), and the Savoy Hotel in London, among others.[2]

These strategies have been adopted globally by organizations seeking the type of competitive advantage that results in superior performance. However, as global competition becomes more intense and organizational performance slips, the effectiveness of these generic strategies must be considered. When considering the effectiveness of these generic competitive strategies, several questions come to mind that may be of managerial interest. Such questions include the following:

- Can managers continue to depend on these strategies to give their organizations a competitive advantage?
- If generic strategies have lost some of their potency, can global competitors attribute reductions in the effectiveness of these strategies to their widespread adoption?
- Have these strategies become such an integral part of organizations' grand strategy that to abandon them will result in a loss of competitive advantage?

Providing answers to these questions is beyond the scope of this book. However, we raise them for the purpose of providing managers with an impetus for moving beyond the confines of these generic strategies and into the realm of corporate culture as a source of competitive advantage.

The Case for Corporate Culture

The concept of distinctive competence is defined as something that an organization does or possesses that empowers it to build a competitive advantage.[3] In this book we view corporate culture as a potential distinctive competence that is, for the most part, overlooked by managers as a source of competitive advantage for the organization. More specifically, we believe that corporate culture plays a central role in the organization's ability to create and sustain a competitive advantage.

Indeed, studies have confirmed the important role corporate culture plays in successful organizations. For example, researchers concluded that Southwest Airline's distinctive competence *is* its corporate culture—a culture that calls for the organization to be committed to providing value to customers in terms of both low cost and differentiated features. Furthermore, it was found that Southwest's competitors have been unable to duplicate this corporate culture-strategy mix.[4]

In another study, researchers examined the successful performance of McKinsey & Co. (recognized as the world's most powerful consulting firm) to see how it sustained its competitive advantage in what is an increasingly fragmented and competitive marketplace for consulting services. After completing their study, the researchers, along with McKinsey's competitors and clients, agreed that McKinsey's corporate culture was the source of its sustainable competitive advantage.[5] Generally speaking, because corporate culture influences how the organization conducts its business and helps regulate and control employees' behavior, it can be a source of competitive advantage.[6]

It has been suggested that for corporate culture to be a source of competitive advantage, it must satisfy three conditions:[7]

- First, it must generate specific value for the organization. In this book we view corporate culture as generating specific value in that it determines whether the organization's strategy will be successfully implemented. In turn, successful strategy implementation determines the financial health of the organization.
- Second, an organization's corporate culture must be unique. Uniqueness ensures that corporate culture is an exclusive advantage for the organization. In Chapter 2 we identify several types of corporate culture that organizations might adopt to ensure uniqueness.
- Third, it must not be easy to imitate. Difficulty of imitation guarantees that the advantages corporate culture provides to the organization will be sustainable over an extended time period. The strategic change approach to aligning organizational subcultures should result in a corporate culture that is not easily imitable, by virtue of each organization's uniqueness.

It has been observed that some corporate cultures are weak and fragmented, in that several subcultures exist and few values are shared organization-wide.[8] There is an increasing body of evidence suggesting that weak corporate cultures are associated with inferior organizational performance, and strong corporate cultures are associated with superior organizational performance.[9] Strong corporate culture increases an organization's ability to create and sustain a competitive advantage.

Moreover, strong corporate culture implies that organizational values are deeply held and widely shared by employees.[10]

Corporate Culture and Values Commitment

Researchers who have conducted extensive studies of corporate culture have found that the more employees are committed to key organizational values, the stronger the organization's corporate culture is.[11] These same researchers suggest that employees in organizations with strong corporate culture are more committed to their organization's values than employees in organizations with weak corporate culture. Both strong and weak corporate cultures have multiple subcultures; however, a key difference is that when corporate culture is strong, subcultures are aligned, whereas when corporate culture is weak, subcultures are misaligned. Findings from these research studies are summarized in Figure 1.1.

The short arrows in the model, leading from corporate culture to subculture alignment and subculture misalignment, indicate that in some organizations there are subgroups within the collective of employees that do not identify with organizational values to the same extent as other subgroups. In these organizations, the corporate culture is fragmented in that many subgroups exist, and only a few organizational values are shared by these subgroups. This is what we mean by subculture: subgroups of employees within the same organization differ in the extent to which they identify with organizational values.

The long arrows in the model depict a correlation between subculture commitment to organizational values and corporate culture. As indicated by the long arrow on the left side of this model, a high level of value commitment produces a strong corporate culture, and a strong corporate culture is indicative of subculture alignment. In contrast, the long arrow on the right side of the model indicates that a low level of value commitment produces a weak corporate culture, which is indicative of subculture misalignment. Finally, the left side of the model shows that the alignment of subcultures results in superior organizational performance, and the right side of the model shows that misalignment of subcultures results in inferior organizational performance.

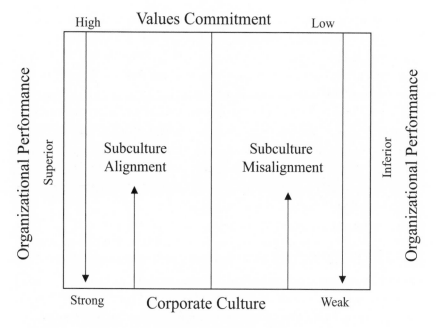

FIGURE 1.1   Commitment, Culture, Performance Relationship

The Role of Organizational Subcultures

Subcultures are a reality in all organizations and may be based on membership in various groups such as departments, work groups, and teams;
levels of hierarchies, such as management versus support staff; professional and occupational affiliations; physical location in the organization; socio-demographic categories such as gender, ethnicity, age, or
nationality; and informal groups like friendship networks. These subcultures are often viewed by management as representing tolerated deviations that do not disrupt the normative solidarity of the overall
corporate culture's dominant values. However, these deviations may become intolerable when there is significant value misalignment among
the various subcultures within the organization. The existence of subcultures virtually guarantees that the predominant value system for the organization as a whole is not likely to be deeply held and widely shared by
each of these subcultures.

For example, departmentalization (that is, dividing the organization into departments such as marketing, accounting, manufacturing, and personnel) in large organizations encourages the development of occupational subcultures whose members tend to share unique values that may not be consistent with the predominant value system of the organization.[12] It is the differences in departments' work orientation, with respect to goals, time, interpersonal relationships, and structure, that promote the formation of distinct values in these subcultures. One must logically conclude that if each occupational subculture within an organization subscribes to a distinct value system, then subculture misalignment is likely to be a problem within the organization.

Increasing diversity in the workforce also has the potential to create ethnic and racial subcultures within organizations. For the most part, these subcultures have their basis in the values of the country from which these diverse individuals originate. In other words, as individuals from different countries join the workforce of a given organization, the value system of their national culture will undoubtedly accompany them. It has been argued that many managers believe that corporate culture will moderate or erase the influence of national culture.[13] However, research has found that employees from different countries bring their cultural affinities to the workplace and tend to maintain and even strengthen their cultural differences.[14] Thus, subcultures based on racial and ethnic backgrounds can potentially weaken corporate culture if alignment is not achieved.

Generational subcultures may also contribute to misalignments within organizations. For example, organization populations can be roughly divided into those employees in their 40s and 50s ("Baby Boomers"), those who are in their late 20s or early 30s ("Generation X"), and those in their early 20s ("Generation Nexters"). Intergenerational conflict among these different age groups is nothing new; however, research suggests that managers of contemporary organizations are complaining about how differences in intergroup values and commitment are affecting organizational performance.[15] Basically, this research suggests that generational subcultures are most harmful when groups of employees are divided by different values—values that are not always consistent with those that define an organization's corporate culture.

Finally, it is widely recognized that male and female employees within organizations value different outcomes and hold different expectations with respect to the workplace. For example, it has been observed that men value power, competency, efficiency, and achievement and that a man's sense of self is defined through his ability to achieve results.[16] In contrast, women are said to value love, communication, beauty, and relationships and that a woman's sense of self is defined by her feelings and the quality of her relationships.[17] In terms of the effects of these value differences on corporate culture, a Conflict Resolution Network news release commentary on Helena Cornelius's book, *The Gentle Revolution*, stated, "We are in the midst of a revolution in the workplace—an enormous social shift in workplace values. Traditional masculine values are giving ground to a new wave of feminine priorities. As women take their point of view into the workforce, work often becomes the battlefield. . . . Sometimes we feel overwhelmed or defeated by the conflict."[18] Suggested by this commentary is that gender subcultures in organizations, if not aligned, can have an adverse impact on corporate culture.

Although subcultures come in many forms in organizations, in this book we will limit our coverage to those that are likely to have the greatest impact on the overall corporate culture. Thus, our focus will be using the strategic change approach to align occupational subcultures, ethnic and racial subcultures, generational subcultures, and gender subcultures within organizations.

The Alignment Imperative

Research is in general agreement that the existence of subcultures within organizations (1) can result in a fragmented and weak corporate culture, (2) can affect organizational performance, and (3) can restrict an organization's capacity to create and sustain a competitive advantage. The argument we build in this book is that subcultures must be aligned if organizations are to achieve and sustain a competitive advantage in the marketplace and realize above-average profits. Other research supports our argument by suggesting that corporate culture can either be a strategic tool or a strategic constraint, depending on the degree to which subcultures within organizations are in alignment.[19]

This research can be interpreted to mean that corporate culture is a strategic tool when it is supportive of organizational strategy and a constraint when it does not support strategy. In confirmation of this interpretation, it has been argued that a strong strategy-supportive corporate culture nurtures and motivates employees to do their jobs in ways conducive to effective strategy execution; it provides structure, standards, and a value system in which to operate; and it promotes strong employee identification with the organization's vision, performance targets, and strategy.[20]

In other words, strong corporate culture promotes good strategy execution when there is a good fit with the strategy and hurts execution when there is a poor fit.[21] Research cited in this book clearly points out the need for corporate culture to support strategy, given the highly competitive global environment in which organizations now must operate. This research also allows managers to draw clear conclusions about why it is imperative that subcultures within organizations are aligned with corporate culture.

Common themes in this research include the following: (1) an organization's ability to successfully implement its strategy is essential to sustaining and improving its long-term market position and competitiveness, (2) a strong corporate culture is essential to successful strategy implementation, and (3) a strong corporate culture is one where subcultures are aligned such that an organization's employees identify with and are committed to the same set of organizational values. In summary, the notion that subcultures must be aligned (the imperative) if organizations expect to create and sustain a competitive advantage is strongly supported by the relationships among corporate culture, strategy, competitive advantage, and organizational performance. These relationships are illustrated in Figure 1.2.

Organizational Types

For the most part, large, diverse organizations with multiple subunits or functional departments should be concerned with the existence of subcultures and their alignment with corporate culture. These large organizations include both for-profit (for example, General Motors, General

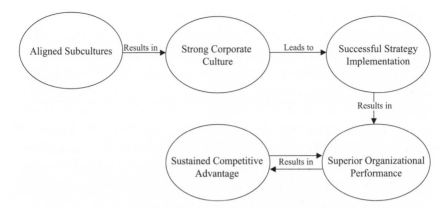

FIGURE 1.2   Effects of Aligned Subcultures

Electric, IBM, Sears, K-Mart, Wal-Mart, Bank of America, McDonald's) and not-for-profit (for example, U.S. Postal Service, Goodwill Industries, University of Colorado, Veterans Administration, United Way) organizations. Some of these large organizations produce goods (for example, automobiles, chairs, clothes, shoes, etc.), and some provide services (for example, restaurants, law firms, banks, hospitals, etc.). Whether these organizations are for-profit or not-for-profit, producers of goods or providers of services, the one thing they have in common is that they are all faced with competition within their respective business environment.

Competitive pressures compel managers of these large organizations to find ways of competing more effectively. Since all of these organizations have their own distinct culture, and their size virtually guarantees that several subcultures exist within their bricks and mortar, there is a high probability that these subcultures are not in precise alignment. If not, such organizations are probably not creating and sustaining a competitive advantage in the marketplace. This book is directed toward these large, diverse organizations, which stand to benefit from subculture alignment.

Individual Types

Aligning organizational subcultures requires change. Like any other type of change in organizations the approach we advocate in this book relies on agents, or individuals who act as catalysts and assume the responsibility for managing the change process. An assumption we make in this book is that the agent responsible for aligning subcultures within organizations will be at least at the manager or director level or an outside consultant. Although it would be desirable for these individuals to have some experience in change management, we make no assumption that they do. Therefore, the agents or individual types we identify in this book are managers who understand the importance of aligning subcultures but possess very little knowledge of how to bring about such an alignment, top managers of organizations who depend heavily on subculture interdependence and total cooperation for strategic success, and consultants and directors of corporate or university-sponsored executive training and development programs.

The Strategic Change Approach

Aligning organizational subcultures requires some type of change to take place. Since this alignment is essentially a cultural change, it may be difficult to accomplish and require interventions that may have ambiguous effects on the organization. Therefore, any type of cultural change that occurs in organizations must be conceptualized and implemented systematically and cautiously. Several useful steps for implementing cultural change have been suggested in the strategic management literature.[22] These steps include the following:

Step 1: Gain a deep understanding of corporate cultures in their various forms (for example, organizational subcultures and their characteristics) and at different levels and locations in the organization.

Step 2: Determine what type of corporate culture is required to successfully implement organizational strategies. (Chapter 2 discusses various types of corporate cultures that organizations might adopt to implement their strategies.) However, these cultures would have to be modified to make them unique to the adopting organization.

Step 3: Identify mismatches between organizational strategies and the existing corporate culture.

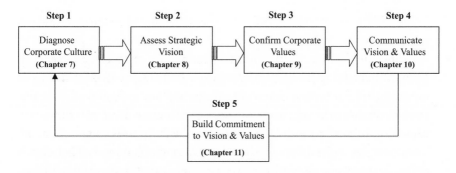

FIGURE 1.3   Model of the Strategic Change Approach

Step 4: Bring to the surface and share the elements of corporate culture identified in Step 1 and Step 2.

Step 5: Change cultural elements (that is, organizational subcultures) by making changes in trigger variables (that is, vision and values).

Step 6: Institutionalize the changes by making them explicit, coding them in organizational policies, giving them the open support of top management, and legitimizing them in practice.

As discussed in later chapters, Step 1, Step 4, Step 5, and Step 6 are important steps in the strategic change approach to aligning organizational subcultures. Although these suggested six steps to implementing cultural change are centered around implementing organizational strategy, we view the strategic change approach as a process that is more vision driven than strategy driven. Our view is based on the notion that a strategic change is motivated by a vision that seeks to move the organization to a "better" state. We also view the strategic change approach as being values driven, in the sense that the change seeks to permeate the organization with values that build the type of team spirit that leads to a strong corporate culture.

The strategic change approach is primarily prescriptive, in that the major topics we discuss focus on those actions the change agent might take to facilitate subculture alignment. Figure 1.3 contains a model of the various steps we feel are essential to the subculture alignment process. Each step in the model represents a chapter in this book, and each is designed to provide insights into how an alignment of subcultures might be brought about.

As indicated in this figure, the strategic change approach begins (Step 1) with diagnosing the corporate culture. Is it fragmented, in the sense that multiple subcultures exist? Are the subcultures aligned with corporate culture? Are the subcultures' values consistent with the predominant value system of the organization? How might these assessments be made? These are the types of questions we answer in Chapter 7. This step is closely aligned with Step 4 of the six steps identified in the strategic management literature, in that actions taken during this step include collecting information. If this information reveals a weak corporate culture, corollary actions include sharing data that show dysfunctional effects of subculture misalignments and providing evidence and plausible explanations to organization members for the necessity of a cultural change.

If the information in Step 1 reveals that organizational subcultures are misaligned, Step 2 in the process (Chapter 8) is to assess the strategic vision of the organization. At this step in the process, we cover various aspects of strategic vision, including vision statement examples, how to make visions effective, and assessments of the appropriateness of the strategic vision for a particular organization. As we mentioned earlier, the process is vision driven, and therefore it is imperative that top managers of organizations first have a clearly articulated strategic vision and assess whether it is appropriate for the organization. If it is not, the assessment process should be repeated until there is consensus concerning its appropriateness.

Once consensus is reached concerning the appropriateness of the strategic vision, Step 3 (Chapter 9) is to confirm corporate values. At this step in the process our focus is on values-based management. What this means is that managers must establish, promote, and practice an organization's values. As we mentioned earlier, the strategic change approach is also values driven, and therefore it is also imperative that organizations confirm their values by clearly establishing what they are, promoting them, and practicing them. If the values cannot be confirmed, this step should be repeated until they are.

Once organizational values have been confirmed, Step 4 (Chapter 10) is to communicate the strategic vision and corporate values. At this step the focus is on identifying the channels of communication and the sources of information and assessing the quality of information sent and received in the organization. In other words, an audit of the organization's communications network is conducted. Once the audit is complete, the actual task of communicating the strategic vision and organizational values is initiated. Methods of initiating and completing this task are explained in Chapter 10.

The task to be completed during Step 5 (Chapter 11) is to build commitment to the strategic vision and corporate values. During this step, the focus is on how to go about gaining commitment. There are several methods and techniques for accomplishing this task. We present these methods and techniques in Chapter 11.

In Chapters 7 through 11, we discuss the strategic change approach in depth, explain what is involved at each step in the process, and provide practical examples for implementing strategic change.

Preview of Conceptual Chapters

The chapters immediately following this introductory chapter (Chapters 2 through 6) are conceptual in nature, in that they consist mainly of discussions and definitions. The purpose of these chapters is to provide you with a conceptual understanding of the relationships among the elements in the model of the strategic change approach (Figure 1.3). These background chapters are also designed to help you better understand the rationale behind this approach to aligning organizational subcultures for competitive advantage.

For example, in Chapter 2 we focus on various aspects of corporate culture. Consistent with Step 1 of the six steps suggested in the strategic management literature, this chapter is designed to help you gain an understanding of organizational cultures in their various forms and at different levels and locations in the organization. Once you have read this chapter you will have a clear understanding of what corporate culture is, what its components are, and how it differs from surrogates such as organizational climate.

In Chapter 3, our discussion focuses on the relationship between corporate culture and organizational performance. First, we define what is meant by the term performance. We then look at various types of strategies that organizations adopt at the corporate level, business level, and functional level to enhance performance. We set forth a conceptual model that describes the relationship among corporate culture, strategy, and performance and discuss empirical studies that provide support for our model. In this chapter the important relationship between corporate culture and the implementation of strategy is also discussed.

In Chapter 4, Chapter 5, and Chapter 6, we elaborate on the types of organizational subcultures briefly discussed at the beginning of this introductory chapter. Specifically, we discuss occupational (Chapter 4), ethnic and racial (Chapter 5), and generational and gender (Chapter 6) subcultures within organizations and provide both theoretical and empirical evidence for considering these groups to be subcultures as opposed to merely conflict-producing groups that affect organizational performance. Once you have read these chapters you will have a clear understanding of the need for the strategic change approach to aligning organizational subcultures.

What Is Corporate Culture?

In Chapter 1, corporate culture was generally defined as the predominant value system for the organization as a whole. While this definition answers the question of what corporate culture is, it does not specifically describe corporate culture. Researchers have identified seven characteristics of corporate culture,[1] which can be viewed as existing on a continuum ranging from low to high:

1. *Individual autonomy.* The degree of responsibility, independence, and opportunity for exercising initiative that individuals in the organization have
2. *Structure.* The number of rules and regulations and the amount of direct supervision that is used to oversee and control employee behavior
3. *Support.* The degree of assistance and warmth provided by managers to their subordinates
4. *Identification.* The degree to which members identify with the organization as a whole rather than with their particular work group or field of professional expertise
5. *Performance reward.* The degree to which reward allocations (for example, salary increase or promotion) are based on employee performance criteria

6. *Conflict tolerance.* The degree of conflict present in relationships between peers and work groups as well as the willingness to be honest and open about differences
7. *Risk tolerance.* The degree to which employees are encouraged to be aggressive, innovative, and risk seeking

Although these characteristics describe corporate culture quite well, it might be argued that the question of what it is could be answered in a more straightforward manner. So what is corporate culture? It has been suggested that employees of organizations can typically describe their respective corporate culture in just a few succinct words. Corporate culture descriptions of some well-known organizations are provided below.[2]

- *Amazon.com.* Described as being loose and easy, exemplified by a very liberal dress and appearance code (for example, body piercing is allowed). The organization's corporate culture is typified by one of its customer service directors telling a temporary employment agency: "Send us your freaks."
- *Exxon/Mobil.* The Exxon part of the organization is described as being reserved, stuffy, buttoned-down, focused on the numbers, controlled, and disciplined. The Mobil part of the organization is described as being feisty, aggressive, and risk taking.
- *DaimlerChrysler.* The Daimler part of the organization is described as being analytical, methodical, disciplined, buttoned-down, and an engineering-driven bureaucracy with conservative styling. The Chrysler part of the organization is described as being impulsive and intuitive, focusing on speedy product development and flashy design.
- *International Business Machines (IBM).* Described as being controlling, powerful, smug, and still hierarchical despite efforts to make the organization more egalitarian and less traditional and conservative. The organization now encourages its employees to wear a wide range of clothing to work.
- *Microsoft.* Described as being adventuresome, creative, and smug, worshipping intelligence, having feelings of superiority, and being

committed to controlling its industry; also described as placing emphasis on problem-solving ability and creativity much more than rank in decision making.

- *Southwest Airlines.* Described as being preoccupied with customer satisfaction, job satisfaction, and laughter on company time, and being intolerant of negative attitudes toward work or customers.

Generally, one might find an answer to the question (what is corporate culture?) by taking the following actions:[3]

1. Observe the physical surroundings of an organization to see how employees are dressed, the degree of openness among offices, the types of pictures and photographs on the walls, the manner in which the workplace is furnished and the placement of the furnishings, and the signs posted throughout the facility.
2. Sit in on a team meeting to see how employees treat each other.
3. Listen to the language employees use to communicate with one another.
4. Note to whom you are introduced and observe how they act.
5. Talk to customers, suppliers, and former employees of the organization to see what they think of the organization.

By taking these actions, one is likely to learn something about the *values* of the organization. This dimension of corporate culture (values) defines what is considered important in the organization.

By taking these suggested actions, one is also likely to learn something about the *identity* of the organization. This dimension of corporate culture communicates what the organization stands for. More specifically, identity reflects the underlying values, assumptions, philosophies, and expectations of organizational life through the use of symbols.

Finally, by taking these actions, one is likely to learn something about the types of *behavior* that are permissible and impermissible within the organization. This dimension of corporate culture provides direction to employees about how things are done in the organization.

Suggested by the foregoing is that corporate culture has three dimensions: values, identity, and behavior. The relationship among these three

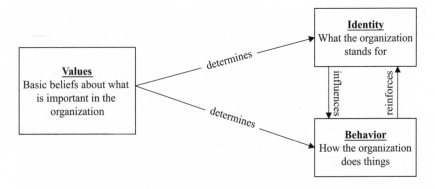

FIGURE 2.1   Dimensions of Corporate Culture

major dimensions of corporate culture is illustrated in Figure 2.1. As shown in this figure, a set of values (that is, what is important) is at the core of every corporate culture. This set of values determines organizational identity (that is, what we stand for) and employee behavior (that is, how we do things). In turn, identity influences behavior and behavior reinforces identity. In this chapter, we will explore each of these dimensions of corporate culture in detail.

The Values Dimension

Corporate culture typically reflects the value system of the organization's founders. However, research on values in new organizations indicates that corporate culture originates from four sources:[4]

1. *Organizational history.* Employees are aware of the organization's past, and this awareness helps to build corporate culture.
2. *External environment.* Because all organizations must interact with their external environment (customers, competitors, suppliers, and so on), the environment has a role in building corporate culture.
3. *Hiring human resources.* Because organizations tend to hire and retain individuals who are similar to employees in their workforce, corporate culture is reinforced as it builds.

4. *Socialization process.* Organizations attach importance to helping new employees adapt to and adopt their corporate culture.

Research has identified five primary and five secondary mechanisms by which corporate culture develops over time,[5] and all of these mechanisms are related to the actions of the executive-level managers in the organization. Executive-level managers help develop corporate culture through five primary mechanisms:

1. By effectively communicating what their vision of the organization is and by informing employees what they want done. The latter is accomplished by consistently emphasizing the same issues in meetings, in casual remarks and questions, and in strategy discussions.
2. By the manner in which they deal with crises. A crisis situation can create new beliefs and values and reveal underlying organizational assumptions.
3. Through deliberate role modeling, teaching, and coaching. The behavior of managers in both formal and informal settings has an important effect on employee beliefs, values, and behaviors.
4. By formulating criteria for the allocation of rewards and status. Managers communicate their priorities and values by consistently linking rewards and punishments to the behaviors they are concerned with.
5. By formulating criteria for recruitment, selection, promotion, and retirement of employees. The types of employees hired by managers are those who accept the organization's values and behave accordingly.

Top managers help develop corporate culture through five secondary mechanisms:

1. Through the organizational structure. Organizational structure offers top managers a chance to express their deeply held assumptions about the tasks facing the organization, the best

means of accomplishing the tasks, human nature, and the right
kinds of relationships among employees.

2. Through organizational systems and procedures. Some very
visible parts of organizational life are the daily, weekly, monthly,
quarterly, and annual cycles of routines, procedures, reports to
file, forms to fill out, and other recurring tasks.

3. Through the design of physical space, facades, and buildings. Top
managers who embrace a clear philosophy and management style
often make that style manifest in their choice of architectural style,
interior design, and décor.

4. Through stories, legends, myths, and parables about important
events and people. As the organization grows and accumulates a
history, some of this history becomes embodied in stories about
events and management behaviors.

5. Through formal statements of organizational philosophy, creeds,
and charters. Explicit statements by top managers about their
values are a means of developing corporate culture.

The last two items in this list are particularly relevant as corporate culture coalesces over time through the telling of stories that reinforce the organization's value system, by the emergence of heroes and heroines who personify corporate values, and by the rites and rituals that reflect corporate values. To illustrate how corporate culture is established, develops, and is sustained over time, we will use the historical time line of Hewlett-Packard (HP).[6] (The time line terminates toward the end of the 1970s, when Bill Hewlett and Dave Packard delegated day-to-day operating management of the company to John Young.)

The time line begins in 1939, when Bill and Dave founded HP in Palo Alto, California. As the company grew during the 1940s, Bill and Dave created a management style that formed the basis of HP's open corporate culture (known as the "HP-Way"), which is marked by personal involvement, good listening skills, and the recognition that "everyone in an organization wants to do a good job." Bill and Dave also established an open door policy to create an atmosphere of trust and mutual understanding.

During the 1950s, Bill and Dave moved HP to its current corporate headquarters in Palo Alto. The new facility supported their personal philosophy that people require attractive and pleasant surroundings to attain maximum job satisfaction and to perform to the best of their abilities. The site includes a landscaped patio, horseshoe pits, volleyball and badminton courts, and a large cafeteria, all for the use of employees.

During the 1960s and 1970s, Bill and Dave pioneered the concept of flexible working hours, which allowed employees to arrive early or late to work as long as they worked a standard number of hours. The original purpose was for HP employees to gain more time for family leisure, conduct personal business, avoid traffic jams, or to satisfy other individual needs. Bill and Dave believed that flextime was the essence of respect for and trust in people.

The HP time line provides insights into the founders' value system (respect for employees), which has become synonymous with HP's corporate culture. The corporate culture at HP has been nurtured, refined, and sustained over time by what are called cultural products.[7] A brief description of each of these cultural products follows:

Rites. Relatively elaborate, dramatic, planned sets of activities that consolidate various forms of cultural expressions into one event, carried out through social interactions, usually for the benefit of an audience.

Ceremonial. A system of several rites connected with a single occasion or event.

Ritual. A standardized, detailed set of techniques and behaviors that manage anxieties, but seldom produce intended, technical consequences of practical importance.

Myth. A dramatic narrative of imagined events usually used to explain origins or transformations of something. Also, an unquestioned belief about the practical benefits of certain techniques and behaviors that is not supported by facts.

Saga. A historical narrative describing the unique accomplishments of a group and its leaders, usually in heroic terms.

Legend. A handed-down narrative of some wonderful event that is based on history but has been embellished with fictional details.

Story. A narrative based on true events, sometimes a combination of truth and fiction.

Folktale. A completely fictional narrative.

Symbol. Any object, act, event, quality, or relation that serves as a vehicle for conveying meaning, usually by representing another thing.

Language. A particular form or manner in which members of a group use sounds and written signs to convey meanings to each other.

Metaphors. Shorthand words used to capture a vision or to reinforce old or new values.

Values. Life-directing attitudes that serve as behavioral guidelines.

Belief. An understanding of a particular phenomenon.

Heroes/Heroines. Individuals whom the organization has legitimized to model behavior for others.

Now, let's return to the Hewlett-Packard time line. After elaborating a little more on four of these cultural products (stories, heroes/heroines, rites, and rituals), we will weave them into this time line.

Stories

These are the oral histories and tales that are told and retold about dramatic events in the life of a corporation and contain narratives of organizational "heroes" or "heroines" who have made significant contributions to the company's success. The "storytellers" range from senior-level managers to nonmanagerial employees who are known as depositories of company history. The stories they tell not only explain the company's heritage but also contain details of milestones that mark individual and company successes.[8]

These stories help employees learn a corporation's culture by anchoring the present in the past, providing explanations and legitimacy for current practices, and exemplifying what is important to the organization. At HP, these stories are about how Bill Hewlett and Dave Packard's personal values of respect for employees are still practiced by managers and still reflected in its corporate culture.[9] They contribute to HP's corporate culture by illustrating and reinforcing important organizational values.

Heroes and Heroines

These individuals are achievers who provide role models for success and contribute to the coalescing of corporate culture by personifying the values of the corporate founders. Bill Hewlett and Dave Packard are foundational heroes of HP because of the pioneering managerial techniques and styles they introduced to the company, including providing catastrophic medical insurance, using first names to address employees (including themselves), and throwing regular employee parties and picnics.

The HP founders' personal values of respect for employees and innovation have been embraced by subsequent CEOs and employees of HP. For example, Lew Platt, who succeeded John Young as CEO, has been recognized inside and outside the company for championing diversity in the workplace, establishing a balance between work and personal life for employees, and directing HP to a leadership position in community involvement. Moreover, in a February 11, 2004, news release, HP officials announced that the pioneering applied scientist and founding director of HP Labs, Barney Oliver, would be inducted into the National Inventors Hall of Fame. In the announcement, the company proclaimed, "During Oliver's 29-year tenure with the company (1952–1981), HP established itself as an icon of excellence in research and development and shaped the face of business in what became known as Silicon Valley. . . . We owe credit to Barney not only for some of the ingenious products that have become inseparable from our everyday lives, but also for the spirit of innovation that still pervades HP and HP Labs today."[10] Dick Lampman, senior vice president of research for HP and director of HP Labs, continued, "We're proud to carry that spirit forward and are dedicated to focusing our research in areas where we can make the greatest contribution to our customers and to society." Heroes such as Lew Platt and Barney Oliver contribute to the coalescing of HP's corporate culture by personifying the values of Bill Hewlett and Dave Packard.

Rites and Rituals

In the business world, rites are ceremonies that celebrate important corporate occasions (for example, product launches or sales conferences), and rituals are management styles and programs that help employees cope with workplace and job issues.

The techniques known as "management by walking around" and "management by objective" (that is, communicating overall objectives clearly and giving employees the flexibility to work toward those goals in ways they determine are best for their own areas of responsibility), which were instituted by Bill Hewlett and Dave Packard, have been ritualized at HP. Management at HP has also ritualized a program called Work/Life Navigation to help employees deal more effectively with workplace and job issues. HP's Web site explains this program as follows:

> Each of us has different needs. As a company, we are committed to developing work/life skills, providing tools, resources and a supportive environment for all our employees. At HP, employees work with their managers to make choices that assist them in navigating their work and personal life challenges while meeting the business needs of the organization. This kind of reciprocal partnership with employees and a flexible work environment has been a hallmark of HP's business success.

Mary Kay Cosmetics provides a good example of rites in organizations. The company's annual "Seminar" (scheduled in four, four-day sessions) is held each July. Before her death, Mary Kay Ash, the corporation's founder, was present at every awards night to personally honor employees for their achievements. Depending on the nature of the award, a consultant (employee) could win a "Mary Kay Pink" Cadillac (first introduced in 1969), a trip, or diamond jewelry. A favorite award among the winners was the Mary Kay porcelain doll dressed in an awards night gown.[11] The Mary Kay and HP examples clearly illustrate that rites and rituals are traditional culture-building events or activities that reflect organizational values and help convert employees to these values.

The Identity Dimension

The second dimension of corporate culture, identity, is manifested in the form of visible symbols of the organization and indicators of organizational life. Representative of such symbols are office décor, norms of dressing, location of key executives' offices, and reserved parking spaces.[12] Organizations may also give employees items such as special ties, blazers, jackets, watches, desk accessories, or office furniture to symbolize status or membership in an exclusive group. These items are carriers of important symbolic cultural messages to employees. Indeed, it has been argued that symbols represent the first layer of corporate culture, comprising the observable artifacts that make up the sensory experience of the organization.[13] It has also been argued that symbols enable employees to home in on corporate culture, because they represent and reveal that which is tacitly known but incommunicable by an organization's members.[14]

Research on symbols suggests that they serve four general functions in organizations:[15]

1. Symbols reflect underlying aspects of corporate culture, generating emotional responses from employees and representing organizational values and assumptions.
2. Symbols elicit internalized norms of behavior, linking employees' emotional responses and interpretations to organizational action.
3. Symbols frame experience, allowing employees to communicate about vague, controversial, or uncomfortable organizational issues.
4. Symbols integrate the entire organization in one system of signification.

As a general rule, symbols are things that can be experienced with the senses and used by employees to make meaning; that is, they are noticed through sight, sound, touch, and smell. Studies cite corporate architecture, organizational landscape, organizational dress, slogans, visual images, metaphors, actions and non-actions, and corporate logos as examples of symbols.[16]

In the case of corporate logos, studies suggest that a logo is a symbol of a company's corporate identity, and through promotion efforts, the company's values, ethics, success or failures, employee satisfaction, customer satisfaction, and all other elements of a company become part of the logo. Thus, when employees and those external to the organization see the logo, they see its identity and corporate culture.

The Behavioral Dimension

Values, which form the core of corporate culture, act as a guide for employee behavior in the workplace. Research has identified several subdimensions of the behavior dimension that give rise to different types of behaviors within organizations.[17] These subdimensions include the following:

- *Innovation and risk taking.* The degree to which employees are encouraged to be innovative and to take risks
- *Attention to detail.* The degree to which employees are expected to exhibit precision, analysis, and attention to detail
- *Outcome orientation.* The degree to which managers focus on results or outcomes rather than on the techniques and processes used to achieve those outcomes
- *People orientation.* The degree to which management decisions take into consideration the effect of outcomes on people within the organization
- *Team orientation.* The degree to which work activities are organized around teams rather than individuals
- *Aggressiveness.* The degree to which people are aggressive and competitive rather than easygoing and cooperative
- *Stability.* The degree to which organizational activities emphasize maintaining the status quo in contrast to growth

In addition to these subdimensions, several studies have developed typologies of corporate culture that provide insight into the behaviors expected of employees. These various typologies and their associated behaviors are outlined below.

Behavioral Typology One

In Deal and Kennedy's book, *Corporate Cultures: The Rites and Rituals of Corporate Life*, the authors identify four types of corporate culture, which they call "corporate tribes."[18] This corporate culture typology includes the "Tough Guy" corporate culture, the "Work-Hard-Play-Hard" corporate culture, the "Bet-the-Company" corporate culture, and the "Process" corporate culture. Each of these cultural types is described below.

Tough Guy Corporate Culture. In this type of corporate culture the value of cooperation is ignored, and there is no opportunity to learn from mistakes. The expected behavior is for employees to tackle tough issues, make complex and difficult deals, and be proactive. Advertising firms, large construction firms, and large movie studios usually subscribe to this type of corporate culture.

Work-Hard-Play-Hard Corporate Culture. Activity is the key to success in this type of corporate culture. The expected behaviors of employees are working long hours and getting rewarded generously for their work. Large sales-oriented organizations subscribe to this type of corporate culture.

Bet-the-Company Corporate Culture. Some organizations subscribe to what researchers call a "bet-the-company" corporate culture that encourages high-risk-taking behaviors. Organizations that typically subscribe to this type of corporate culture include capital goods companies, oil companies, investment banks, and architectural firms.

Process Corporate Culture. Employees in this type of corporate culture are expected to focus on the way things are done rather than on the outcome of what is done. Subsequently, employees tend to be orderly, punctual, and detail-oriented. Banks, insurance companies, government agencies, and utility companies tend to subscribe to this type of corporate culture.

Behavioral Typology Two

Carter McNamara provides a summary of four different types of corporate cultures and suggests the types of organizations in which these types of cultures are likely to be found.[19] For example, he suggests that organizations might subscribe to the following types of culture:

Academy culture. Universities, hospitals, and large corporations are likely to foster this type of corporate culture. These organizations tend to hire experts who are willing to make a slow, steady climb up the corporate ladder, and provide a stable environment to facilitate their climb.

Baseball team culture. Investment banking and advertising firms, which typically face a rapidly changing environment, tend to subscribe to this type of corporate culture. This is considered a high-risk culture because these types of firms hire employees who can best be described as "free agents" with highly sought-after skills.

Club culture. This type of corporate culture is usually found in the military and some law firms, because they tend to have loyal and committed people who usually start their careers at the lower ranks and stay with the firm throughout their career.

Fortress culture. Automobile manufacturers and savings and loan institutions foster this type of culture, because their focus is usually on survival and dealing with declining or stagnant profitability.

Behavioral Typology Three

In yet another typology, Ernest identified four types of corporate culture and specified behavior associated with each type.[20] This typology includes the "interactive" corporate culture, the "integrated" corporate culture, the "entrepreneurial" corporate culture, and the "systematized corporate culture.

Interactive Corporate Culture. The expected behavior in this type of corporate culture is cultivating positive employee relationships and satisfying the needs of the organization's customers. Providing good service is a hallmark of employee behavior.

Integrated Corporate Culture. Cultivating positive employee relationships and satisfying customer needs are also expected behavior in this type of corporate culture; however, being innovative, with respect to developing new products or services, is also expected behavior.

Entrepreneurial Corporate Culture. Being innovative is also expected behavior in this type of corporate culture; however, this type of corporate culture fosters a low orientation toward employee participation in decision making.

Systematized Corporate Culture. Behavior in this type of corporate culture is focused on maintaining procedures, policies, and systems of ongoing activities.

Behavioral Typology Four

Cameron and Quinn developed a corporate culture typology that is built upon a theoretical model called the "Competing Values Framework."[21] The framework is based on four dominant corporate culture types: clan, adhocracy, market, and hierarchy. Associated with each of these corporate culture types are five corporate culture dimensions: dominant characteristic, management of employees, organizational glue, strategic emphases, and criteria of success. These dimensions provide a more comprehensive view of the behaviors that are likely to take place under each corporate culture type. General characteristics of each corporate culture type are provided below, and the dimensions associated with corporate culture type are listed in Table 2.1.

Clan Corporate Culture. In this type of corporate culture, expected employee behavior is directed toward internal maintenance with flexibility, a concern for people, and sensitivity to the organization's customers.

Hierarchy Corporate Culture. In this type of corporate culture, employee behavior is directed toward internal maintenance with a need for stability and control.

Adhocracy Corporate Culture. In this type of corporate culture, employee behavior is directed toward concentrating on external positioning with a high degree of flexibility and individuality.

Market Corporate Culture. In this type of corporate culture, employee behavior is directed toward external maintenance with a need for stability and control.

TABLE 2.1 Corporate Culture Typology and Associated Dimensions

DIMENSIONS

TYPOLOGY	Dominant Characteristics	Management of Employees	Organizational Glue	Strategic Emphases	Criteria of Success
Clan culture	Personal place, extended family; people share a lot of themselves	Teamwork, consensus, participation	Loyalty and mutual trust; organizational commitment runs high	Human development, trust, openness, participation	HRD (personal) development, teamwork, commitment
Adhocracy culture	Very dynamic, entrepreneurial; people willing to take risks	Individual risk taking, innovation, freedom, and uniqueness	Commitment to innovation and development, "cutting edge"	Acquiring new resources, trying new things	Having most unique or newest products, "cutting edge"
Market culture	Very results-oriented; people are competitive, achievement-oriented	Hard-driving competitiveness, high demands, and achievement	Achievement and goal accomplishment; aggressiveness, winning	Competitive actions, achievements, stretch targets, winning in market	Winning in the marketplace and outpacing the competition
Hierarchy culture	Very controlled and structured; formal procedures govern people	Security of employment, conformity, predictability, stability	Formal rules and policies; smooth-running organization is important	Stability, efficiency, control, and smooth operations are important	Efficiency, smooth scheduling, low-cost production

These typologies, in aggregate, capture the essence of the behavior dimension of corporate culture. Specifically, they suggest the range of behavioral norms that can exist in organizations with unique corporate cultures. They also provide insight into the values (for example, acceptable behavior) at the core of each type of corporate culture. These values, in turn, act as a guide for employee behavior within the organization.

The Cultural Network

While the strategic change approach to aligning organizational subcultures consists of tangible and definable tasks, the degree to which subcultures become aligned is influenced by the organization's cultural network.

This network is an aspect of what is called social information processing.[22] The notion behind social information processing is that individuals, as adaptive organisms, adapt attitudes, behaviors, and beliefs consistent with their social context and with their own personal past and present reality.

Essentially, the cultural network is the informal interaction among employees, and it acts as the "carrier" of organizational values. Through the cultural network, values, heroes, and rituals are reinforced, elaborated on, clarified, and qualified. The result is that the network, along with the strategic change approach, produces both cultural intensity and cultural integration, which, in turn, creates a strong (aligned) corporate culture.

Corporate Culture versus Corporate Climate

At this point, you should have a conceptual idea of what corporate culture is. To "capstone" your understanding, let's explore what corporate culture is not. Contrary to the beliefs of many academicians and management practitioners, corporate culture is not what is called corporate climate. Although the two concepts are often used interchangeably, they are not the same. What distinguishes corporate culture from corporate climate? Values are the primary and most important difference between the two concepts.

Although values are at the core of corporate culture and can be viewed as the mortar that holds it together, corporate climate has no identifiable core. It is fragmented and more about how employees feel about their jobs, their supervisors, their peers, top management, and so on than about the internal values that provide them with a sense of corporate identity. Characterized as such, corporate climate can be thought of as being temporal and subjective, and therefore, subject to direct manipulation by management. In contrast, corporate culture is rooted in history, collectively held, and sufficiently complex to resist attempts at direct manipulation by management.[23]

The strategic change approach to aligning organizational subcultures requires that clear distinctions be made between corporate culture and corporate climate before it is implemented. The rationale is based on the desired end result of implementing the strategic change approach to aligning organizational subcultures. In other words, changing corporate climate will not necessarily result in a strong (aligned) corporate culture. However, changes in corporate culture can have a profound effect on corporate climate.

Chapter Summary and Conclusions

Corporate culture can be briefly summarized as follows:

- Corporate cultures are value-laden; they reflect the values of those in the culture.
- Corporate cultures are historical; they develop over time.
- Corporate cultures are persistent; they exist for a long time.
- Corporate cultures grow and change; they change slowly, but they do change.
- Corporate cultures are multilateral; they are influenced by all organizational members.
- Corporate cultures are conservative; they reject elements that threaten the culture.
- Corporate cultures are pluralistic; they can account for diverse or even contradictory roles within a single, coherent whole.
- Corporate cultures exert influence; they tell employees what they are supposed to do.
- Corporate cultures act as discriminators; they make meanings for some and repel others.

The main points presented in this chapter include the following: (1) There are three main dimensions of corporate culture (values, identity, and behavior); (2) values define what is important in organizations and are at the core of corporate culture; (3) values determine what an organization stands for (that is, its identity); and (4) values determine how things are done (that is, behavior) in organizations.

These points suggest that while identity and behavior are important dimensions of corporate culture, values are the glue that holds it together. Therefore, a strong corporate culture (that is, one in which subcultures are aligned) is best achieved by focusing managerial efforts on building a system of shared values throughout the organization. The organization's cultural network represents this system.

Corporate Culture and Performance

The model shown in Figure 3.1 summarizes our discussions up to this point. This model asserts that (1) greater success in implementing organizational strategy leads to superior organizational performance and thus the ability to sustain a competitive advantage in the marketplace, and less success in implementing organizational strategy leads to inferior organizational performance and thus the inability to sustain a competitive advantage; (2) a strong corporate culture leads to greater success in implementing organizational strategy, and a weak corporate culture leads to less success in implementing organizational strategy; and (3) a strong corporate culture is one where subcultures are aligned such that there is greater commitment to the same set of organizational values, and a weak corporate culture is one where subcultures are misaligned such that there is less commitment to the same set of organizational values.

Up to this point, you should have a clear understanding of what corporate culture is and what it is not. What might not be clear is the specific nature of the relationship between corporate culture and organizational performance. As indicated in Figure 3.1, corporate culture affects organizational performance indirectly through its effect on strategy implementation. In this chapter we will examine this relationship more closely. We begin by defining what we mean by organizational performance. We then delve more deeply into the concept of strategy and its relationship to

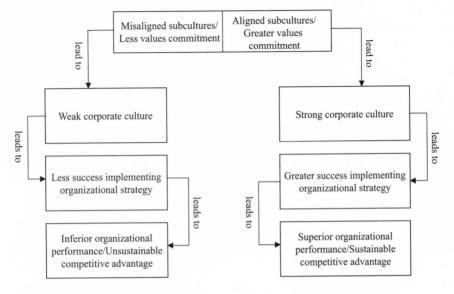

FIGURE 3.1   Summary Model

performance and corporate culture. Next, we look at the relationship between corporate culture and strategy implementation. Finally, we look at the role that commitment to organizational values plays in the relationship between corporate culture and organizational performance.

Organizational Performance

What do we mean by organizational performance? In general terms, organizational performance can be viewed as the accumulated end results of all the organization's work processes and activities.[1] In more specific terms, we view organizational performance as the outcomes of the strategy that an organization implements. From an organization-wide perspective, there are two performance yardsticks that are outcomes of strategy implementation. One yardstick relates to an organization's *financial performance* and the other relates to an organization's *strategic performance*.[2] It has been argued that achieving satisfactory financial performance by itself is not enough; managers must also pay attention to the organization's strategic well-being (for example, its competitiveness and overall long-term business position).[3] In other words, unless an organization's performance reflects improving competitive strength and long-term market position, it will be constrained in its ability to continue delivering superior financial performance.

Some representative measures/indicators of strong financial performance include the following:[4]

- Revenue growth
- Earnings growth
- Larger profit margins
- Higher returns on invested capital
- Strong bond and credit ratings
- Larger cash flows
- Rising stock price
- A more diversified revenue base
- Stable earnings during periods of recession

Some representative measures/indicators of strong strategic performance include the following:[5]

- A larger market share
- Higher levels of customer satisfaction
- A stronger brand name
- Higher product/service quality
- Faster product development-to-market times
- Stronger global distribution capabilities
- Wider geographic coverage
- More attractive product/service line

Four commonly used measures of financial performance are shown in Figure 3.2. As indicated in this figure, these four measures include return on investment (ROI), return on equity (ROE), return on sales (ROS), and earnings per share (EPS). These measures are called profitability ratios, and they indicate how well an organization's resources are being allocated. For example, ROI focuses on the profitability of the overall operation of the firm. It is the single most important measure of an

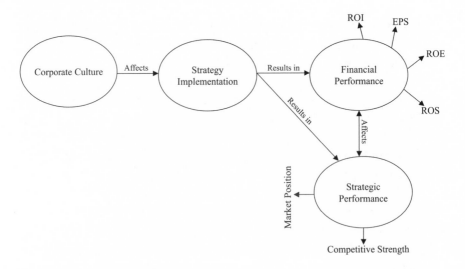

FIGURE 3.2   Culture-Strategy-Performance Relationship

organization's financial position and allows management to measure the effects of its strategy on the organization's profitability.

ROE reveals how much profit an organization earns in comparison to the total amount of equity shareholders have in the organization. An organization that has a high return on equity is more likely to be one that is capable of generating cash internally and therefore increasing the wealth of its shareholders. In short, this ratio tells managers whether all the effort put into the organization has been worthwhile. ROS reveals how much profit an organization makes for every dollar it generates in revenue. The higher an organization's ROS compared to its competitors, the better. EPS evaluates the profitability and success of an organization on a per-share basis. Generally, it measures the per-share dollar return to shareholders of an organization.

As shown in Figure 3.2, one important measure of strategic performance is an organization's competitive strength. Signs of competitive strength and competitive weakness have been identified as follows:[6]

• *Signs of competitive strength.* Important core competencies; strong market share (or a leading market share); a pacesetting or distinctive strategy; growing customer base and customer loyalty;

above-average market visibility; in a favorably situated strategic group; concentrating on fastest-growing market segments; strongly differentiated products; cost advantages; above-average profit margins; above-average technological and innovational capability; a creative, entrepreneurially alert management; in a position to capitalize on opportunities.

- *Signs of competitive weakness.* Confronted with competitive disadvantages; losing ground to rival firms; below-average growth in revenues; short on financial resources; a slipping reputation with customers; trailing in product development; in a strategic group destined to lose ground; weak in areas where there is the most market potential; a higher-cost producer; too small to be a major factor in the marketplace; not in a good position to deal with emerging threats; weak product quality; lacking skill and capabilities in key areas.

Another important measure of strategic performance, as indicated in Figure 3.2, is market position. It has been suggested that there are at least three factors that determine an organization's position in the market-place.[7] The first factor is the number of competitors that currently exist in the marketplace. If there are a large number of competitors and the level of competition is high, strategy has to be well defined and supportive to ensure market share. The second factor is width of customer base. If the customer base is small, market position is likely to be weak. The third factor is vulnerability to sudden changes in economic, social, technological, or political conditions. If the organization is vulnerable, market position is likely to be weak.

In concluding our discussion of organizational performance, we would be remiss if we failed to speak to the notion of measuring performance in not-for-profit organizations. The financial and strategic performance measures we discuss in this section apply to for-profit organizations and are not applicable to not-for-profit organizations. The lack of a profit motive makes measuring performance in not-for-profit organizations very difficult, although it is not impossible. The extent to which the public interest is met and political efficiency are often regarded as the most important measures of performance in not-for-profit organizations.[8] However, neither of these measures is well defined, and both rely on the subjective judgment of various stakeholders as to the level of performance.

Strategy, Performance, and Corporate Culture

Now that we have operationally defined what we mean by organizational performance, let's look at the variable (strategy) that has been identified as having a direct effect on financial and strategic performance. The concept of strategy can be defined as the guiding idea of an organization or an expression of how the organization has operated, or intends to operate, in a competitive environment.[9] Although this definition is general, it captures the essence of strategy. However, in more specific terms, strategy outlines the fundamental actions that an organization intends to take in order to achieve an objective or set of objectives.[10] We adopt this more specific definition in our references to strategy in this book.

As discussed in Chapter 1, Michael Porter identified three generic organizational strategies: *cost-leadership* (producing goods or services at a cost lower than competitors), *differentiation* (creating a product or service that is perceived by customers to be unique in some important way), and *focus* (concentrating on serving a particular market niche).[11] These generic strategies are generally classified as *business-unit strategies,* and they focus on how to compete in a given business. Business-unit strategies are narrower in scope than another classification of strategies, called *corporate strategies,* in that they apply to a single business unit.

Corporate strategies are established at the top-management level of the organization and involve a long-range time horizon; they consist of three types. The first type is called a *stable growth strategy,* in that organizations take fundamental actions that are designed to pursue the same or similar set of objectives; this is because such organizations are satisfied with their past performance. There are three types of stable growth strategies: (1) *concentration,* in which organizations direct their resources to the profitable growth of a narrowly defined product and market, focusing on a dominant technology; (2) *market development,* in which organizations market their present products, often with only cosmetic modifications, to customers in related market areas by adding channels of distribution or by changing the content of advertising or promotion; and (3) *product development,* in which organizations substantially modify their existing products or create new but related products that can be marketed to their current customers through established channels.

Stable growth strategies can be generally characterized as follows:[12]

- Organizations grow by maintaining their share of a steadily increasing market.
- Organizations grow by slowly increasing their share of the market.
- Organizations grow by adding new products or services.
- Organizations grow by expanding their market coverage geographically.

The second type of corporate strategy is called a *growth strategy,* in that organizations take fundamental actions that allow them to grow faster than the markets in which their products or services are sold. There are six types of growth strategies: (1) *innovation,* in which organizations seek to reap the initially high profits associated with customer acceptance of a new or greatly improved product and then, rather than face stiffening competition, search for other original or novel ideas; (2) *horizontal integration,* in which organizations acquire one or more similar organizations operating at the same stage of the production-marketing chain; (3) *vertical integration,* in which organizations acquire other organizations that supply it with inputs *(backward vertical integration)* or that are customers for its outputs *(forward vertical integration)*; (4) *joint venture,* in which organizations form strategic alliances with other organizations for the purpose of sharing resources to exploit an opportunity that a single organization cannot exploit with its own resources; (5) *concentric diversification,* in which organizations acquire or internally generate a separate business with synergistic possibilities counterbalancing the strengths and weaknesses of the two businesses; and (6) *conglomerate diversification,* in which organizations acquire a business because it represents the most promising investment opportunity available.

Growth strategies can be generally characterized as follows:[13]

- Organizations grow by choosing a field of business that is expanding more rapidly than the economy as a whole.
- Organizations grow by choosing a specific subsector that is growing even more rapidly than the general field of business.
- Organizations grow by choosing a rapidly expanding market segment served by the specific subsector.
- Organizations grow by choosing a specific subsector that is at an earlier stage of economic growth than the general field of business.
- Organizations grow by using internal expansion, mergers, and acquisitions.
- Organizations grow by entering foreign markets.

The third type of corporate strategy is called a *retrenchment strategy*, in that organizations take fundamental actions designed to enable them to weather bad economic times. There are three types of retrenchment strategies: (1) *turnaround*, in which organizations try to reduce operating costs either by cutting "excess fat" and operating more efficiently or by reducing the size of their operations; (2) *divestiture*, in which organizations either sell themselves to another organization as a going concern or sell a major component of the organization; and (3) *liquidation*, in which organizations go out of business by selling off parts of the organization for their tangible asset value and not as a going concern.

Retrenchment strategies can be generally characterized as follows:

- Organizations cut back on capital expenditures.
- Organizations centralize decision making in an attempt to control costs.
- Organizations cut back on hiring new personnel.
- Organizations reduce advertising and promotion expenditures.
- Organizations engage in general belt-tightening, including the firing of some personnel.
- Organizations increase emphasis on cost control and budgeting.
- Organizations sell off some assets.
- Organizations tighten inventory control.
- Organizations improve the collection of accounts receivable.

Another major category of organizational strategies is called *functional-level strategies*. These strategies are narrower in scope than *business-unit strategies* and are concerned with the activities of the different functional areas of an organization such as production/operations, finance, personnel, and marketing. Generally, functional-level strategies support business-unit strategies and are adopted for a relatively short period of time (usually one year or less) and are primarily concerned with "how to" issues.

For example, *production/operations strategy* is concerned with taking fundamental actions related to selecting, designing, and updating the systems that produce the organization's products or services and with operating those systems.[14] *Financial strategy* is concerned with taking two types of fundamental actions—those related to acquiring funds to meet the current and future needs of the organization, and those related to recording, monitoring, and controlling the financial results of the organization's operations.[15] *Personnel strategy* is concerned with taking fundamental actions related to determining the human resources needed to achieve the organization's objectives,[16] and *marketing strategy* is concerned with taking fundamental actions related to moving products or services from the producer to the consumer or market.

Whether they are functional-level, business-level, or corporate-level strategies, each requires a supportive corporate culture if they are to be effective in achieving the organization's performance goals. Indeed, it has been stated:[17]

- A work environment where the corporate culture matches the conditions for good strategy implementation provides a system of informal rules and peer pressure regarding how to conduct business internally and how to go about doing one's job.
- A strong strategy-supportive corporate culture nurtures and motivates people to do their jobs in ways conducive to effective strategy implementation; it provides structure, standards, and a value system in which to operate; and it promotes strong employee identification with the organization's vision, performance targets, and strategy.

Implied in these statements is that a strategy-supportive corporate culture shapes the mood, temperament, and motivation of the workforce, positively affecting organizational energy, work habits, and operating practices; the degree to which organizational units cooperate; and how customers are treated.[18] Alternatively, in organizations where strategy and culture are misaligned, ingrained subculture values do not cultivate strategy-supportive ways of operating, and often the types of behavior needed to successfully implement strategy are contrary to the types of behavior fostered by the dominant value system within the organization.[19]

Corporate Culture and Strategy Implementation

Strategy implementation can be viewed as the process of translating strategy into the types of actions that result in organizational performance.[20] A corporate culture grounded in values that match what is needed for successful strategy implementation helps to energize employees throughout the organization to do their jobs in a strategy-supportive manner. With respect to the types of strategies identified by Porter, a culture where frugality and thrift are values strongly shared by organizational subcultures will lead to the successful implementation of a cost-leadership strategy.[21] Similarly, corporate cultures in which creativity, embracing change, and challenging the status quo are dominant values will lead to product innovation and the successful implementation of a technological leadership strategy. A corporate culture that values listening to customers, encouraging employees to take pride in their work, and giving employees a high degree of decision-making autonomy will lead to the successful implementation of a superior customer service strategy.[22]

These examples suggest that corporate culture can be either a strategic tool or a strategic constraint, depending on the degree to which subcultures within organizations are in alignment and are supportive of organizational strategy. Two examples demonstrate the importance of subcultures being in alignment and supportive of organizational strategy. The first comes from the oil industry and focuses on what is called the "executives" and the "operators" subcultures. These two subcultures are discussed in detail in Chapter 4.

The CEOs ("executives" subculture) of two major oil companies determined that they would have to diversify out of oil (strategy) because their current business could not support long-term growth and faced serious political threats. Not only did the two CEOs announce their strategies to employees ("operators" subculture), but they established elaborate plans to implement them. Neither of the CEOs was able to implement his strategy, not because the strategy was ill conceived or theoretically inappropriate, but because neither had understood that his company's culture was so entrenched in the traditions and values of doing business as oilmen that employees resisted (and sabotaged) the strategy.[23]

The second example relates to the potential impact of racial and ethnic subcultures on attempts to implement strategy in high-tech companies. These subcultures are discussed in detail in Chapter 5.

Because high-tech companies face short product cycles, their corporate culture is typically characterized by values that foster *individual autonomy* (that is, employees are expected to exhibit responsibility, independence, and initiative) and *risk tolerance* (that is, employees are expected to be aggressive, innovative, and risk seeking). Consequently, the strategies implemented by high-tech companies rely heavily on employees who possess similar values. However, as we demonstrate in Chapter 5, racial and ethnic subcultures in U.S. organizations do not necessarily subscribe to these values.

Geert Hofstede, a noted researcher, conducted an extensive study on the values of various cultural groups[24] and classified the work-related values of racial and ethnic cultural groups into four characteristic dimensions:

- *Power distance* is the degree to which employees accept inequalities in organizational relationships. Employees from high power distance countries expect inequalities to exist in organizations, and employees from low power distance countries expect equal opportunity to exist in organizations.
- *Individualism* is the degree to which employees view themselves as individuals or part of the larger organization. Employees from high individualist countries tend to exhibit more individual autonomy than employees from low individualist countries.

- *Masculinity* is the degree to which employees exhibit assertiveness and materialism versus concern for people and quality of life. Employees from high masculinity countries expect there to be a high degree of gender differentiation in organizations, and employees from low masculinity countries expect females to be treated equally to males in organizations.
- *Uncertainty avoidance* is the degree to which employees feel threatened by situations that are unstructured, unclear, or unpredictable. Employees from high uncertainty avoidance countries expect organizations to have clear rules, policies, and controls in order to reduce the amount of uncertainty. Employees from low uncertainty avoidance countries are less rule oriented, accept change more readily, and take more and greater risks.

Hofstede found that the work-related values and employee characteristics outlined in Tables 3.1, 3.2, 3.3, and 3.4 vary among different cultural groups. First, power distance tends to be high in employees from Latin American cultural clusters (for example, Argentina, Chile, Colombia, Mexico, Peru, and Venezuela) and high in Far Eastern cultural clusters (for example, China, Hong Kong, Indonesia, Japan, Malaysia, Philippines, Singapore, Taiwan, Thailand, and Vietnam). Second, individualism is de-emphasized (low) in both Latin American and Far Eastern cultural clusters. Third, uncertainty avoidance is emphasized (high) in Latin American cultural clusters and Far Eastern cultural clusters. There are no significant differences between the Latin American and Far Eastern cultural clusters on the masculinity/femininity dimension.

Employees in U.S. high-tech companies are expected to take individual initiative, take independent action, and to be aggressive and risk-takers to successfully implement strategy. These expectations are consistent with the corporate culture of such companies. However, subcultures of employees from the Latin American cultural cluster and subcultures of employees from the Far Eastern cultural cluster may be reluctant to take initiative because of their lower position in the hierarchy (high power distance), to take risks (high uncertainty avoidance), and to exhibit individual autonomy (low individualism).

TABLE 3.1   Power Distance Characteristics in Organizations

Low Power Distance Cultures	*High Power Distance Cultures*
1. Employees are less afraid to disagree with their managers	1. Employees fear disagreeing with their managers
2. Employees are more cooperative	2. Employees reluctant to trust each other
3. Higher-educated employees hold much less authoritarian values than lower educated ones	3. High- and lower-educated employees show similar values about authority
4. Mixed feelings about employees' participation in management	4. Ideological support for employees' participation in management
5. Close supervision negatively evaluated by subordinates	5. Close supervision positively evaluated by subordinates
6. Stronger perceived work ethic among employees	6. Weaker perceived work ethic among employees
7. Managers more satisfied with participative superior	7. Managers more satisfied with directive or persuasive superior
8. More consideration among managers	8. Less consideration among managers
9. Subordinates' preference for managers' decision-making style clearly centered on consultative, give-and-take style	9. Subordinates' preference for managers' decision-making style polarized between autocratic-paternalistic and majority rule

Source: Adapted from G. Hofstede, *Culture's Consequences: International Differences in Work-Related Values* (Newbury Park, Calif.: Sage, 1984), p. 92.

TABLE 3.2 Individualism and Collectivism
Characteristics in Organizations

Individualistic Cultures	*Collectivist Cultures*
1. Employees are emotionally independent from the company	1. Employees are emotionally dependent on the company
2. More importance attached to freedom and challenge in jobs	2. More importance attached to training and use of skills in jobs
3. Managers aspire to leadership	3. Managers aspire to conformity
4. Managers rate having autonomy as being more important	4. Managers rate having security as being more important
5. Individual decisions are considered better than group decisions	5. Group decisions are considered better than individual decisions
6. Managers choose pleasure, affection, and security as life goals	6. Managers choose duty, expertise, and prestige as life goals
7. Employee initiative is encouraged	7. Employee initiative is frowned upon
8. Fewer years of schooling needed to do a given job	8. More years of schooling needed to do a given job
9. Employees attracted to small companies	9. Employees attracted to large companies

SOURCE: Adapted from G. Hofstede, *Culture's Consequences: International Differences in Work-Related Values* (Newbury Park, Calif.: Sage, 1984), p. 92.

TABLE 3.3   Masculine/Feminine Characteristics in Organizations

Masculine Cultures	*Feminine Cultures*
1. Greater value differences between men and women in the same jobs	1. Smaller or no value differences between men and women in the same jobs
2. Managers less attracted to service role	2. Managers have more of a service ideal
3. Achievement defined in terms of recognition and wealth	3. Achievement defined in terms of human contacts and living environment
4. Greater work centrality	4. Work less central in people's lives
5. Company's interference in employees' private life is accepted	5. Company's interference in employees' private life is rejected
6. Employees prefer more salary to shorter working hours	6. Employees prefer shorter working hours to more salary
7. Stronger achievement motivation among employees	7. Weaker achievement motivation among employees
8. Managers more interested in leadership, independence, and self-realization	8. Managers less interested in leadership, independence, and self-realization
9. Earnings, recognition, advancement, and challenge relatively more important	9. Relationship with manager, cooperation, friendly work environment, and employment security more important

SOURCE: Adapted from G. Hofstede, *Culture's Consequences: International Differences in Work-Related Values* (Newbury Park, Calif.: Sage, 1984), p. 92.

TABLE 3.4   Uncertainty Avoidance
Characteristics in Organizations

Low Uncertainty Avoidance Cultures	*High Uncertainty Avoidance Cultures*
1. Employee optimism about motives behind company activities	1. Employee pessimism about motives behind company activities
2. Company rules may be broken for pragmatic reasons	2. Company rules should not be broken for any reason
3. Loyalty to employer is not seen as a virtue	3. Loyalty to employer is seen as a virtue
4. Lower average age in higher-level jobs	4. Higher average age in higher-level jobs
5. Stronger achievement motivation	5. Weaker achievement motivation
6. Competition between employees can be fair and right	6. Competition between employees is emotionally disapproved of
7. Acceptance of foreigners as managers	7. Suspicion toward foreigners as managers
8. More employee risk taking	8. Less employee risk taking
9. Hope of success among employees	9. Fear of failure among employees

SOURCE: Adapted from G. Hofstede, *Culture's Consequences: International Differences in Work-Related Values* (Newbury Park, Calif.: Sage, 1984), p. 92.

As we discuss in Chapter 5, new entrants to the U.S. workforce come primarily from Latin American and Far Eastern cultural clusters. However, the work-related values of employees from Latin American and Asian countries are not likely to be aligned with the values needed by U.S. high-tech companies—namely, individual autonomy and risk tolerance—for successful strategy implementation.

These two examples suggest that as a strategic tool, corporate culture promotes successful strategy implementation when there is fit with the strategy, and conversely, corporate culture inhibits successful implementation when there is little fit with the strategy. The notion of "fit" suggests that employees are an important part of the strategy implementation process. Strategy requires various activities to be performed, and for many of these activities, there are no explicit rules for performing them. Therefore, employees rely on corporate culture as a source of guidance.[25] Corporate culture gives employees a sense of what they should do and where to place priorities in carrying out these activities.[26] In this sense, corporate culture is a valuable tool for implementing strategy.

The significance of corporate culture in implementing strategy, then, is the guidance it affords employees as they go about the task of executing strategy-related activities. Evidence indicates that a strong corporate culture (one in which subcultures are aligned) provides clearer guidance and thus more positively impacts employee behaviors that are related to successful strategy implementation.[27]

The Role of Values Commitment

It has been theorized that the nature of employees' commitment to the dominant value system of organizations affects two distinct, ongoing decisions. The first is whether they will participate in organizational activities (for example, strategy implementation), and the second is whether they will perform at the level necessary to successfully carry out these activities.[28] Decisions that relate to whether employees will perform at necessary levels are most relevant to the implementation of an organization's strategy. Research studies have identified four major components of this decision.[29]

1. A sense of internalization in which employees find the values of the organization to be congruent with their personal values.
2. A sense of identification with the organization's objectives such that employee and organizational goals are closely aligned.
3. A sense of involvement and psychological immersion in one's work resulting in considerable enjoyment.
4. A sense of loyalty, perhaps even affection, toward the organization as a place to spend one's time and work.

This research suggests that these components tend to be associated with those employees who not only trust their organization but also have a clear understanding of what they are expected to do. Strong corporate cultures provide this understanding. Moreover, employees with a high level of commitment to organizational values not only provide the organization with a stable and secure workforce, and thus a strong corporate culture, but make the implementation of the organization's strategy more effective as well.[30]

Chapter Summary and Conclusions

This chapter has described (1) the different types of organizational performance (financial and strategic) and how they are measured; (2) the different types of strategies (corporate, business-unit, and functional); and (3) the relationship among corporate culture, strategy implementation, and organizational performance. A major point of this chapter is that corporate culture must be aligned with and supportive of organization strategy for strategy to be successfully implemented.

This chapter provided a preview of how different organizational subcultures can potentially affect the implementation of organizational strategy if not properly aligned. In Chapter 4, Chapter 5, and Chapter 6 we delve more deeply into the value systems of occupational subcultures, racial and ethnic subcultures, and gender and generational subcultures.

Occupational Subcultures

To begin this chapter, we look at some general typologies of occupational subcultures. The first typology contains three different types of occupational subcultures that exist in every organization: the "operators" subculture, the "engineers" subculture, and the "executives" subculture.[1] The "operators" subculture is the set of values held by the employees who deliver the products and services that fulfill the organization's basic mission. The culture of operators evolves locally in an organization or unit and is based on human interaction. Members of this occupational subculture discover the systemic interdependencies among the functional areas of the organization and learn to deal with them. As a result, they may use their learning ability to thwart management's efforts to improve productivity.

The "engineers" subculture is viewed as being composed of "technocrats," where the basic values they subscribe to are heavily skewed toward systems, machines, routines, and processes, not people. From members of this subculture's perspective, every organization can be made totally reliable and automatic. The "executives" subculture is composed of top managers whose values are focused on sustaining profitability and increasing shareholder returns. Thus, members of this subculture generally believe that reward and control systems are the keys to organizational success. A point of misalignment between members of the "executives" and the "engineers" subcultures is their disagreement on how to make organizations work better while keeping costs down.

In a study of subcultures in a medium-sized conglomerate in the United States, Sonja Sackman found that the conglomerate's production division consisted of three occupational subcultures: electronics production, shop floor production, and product inspection.[2] Sackman described the subcultures in the following way:

> Each subgroup was influenced by the nature of its particular work. This "local" orientation also differentiated each group from the others. All three groupings clearly distinguished between "we" and "them." This distinction was supported by my observations of them. They dressed differently, and they worked in distinctly different work spaces that were furnished differently. They took separate breaks during the day, and the tone in which they interacted varied in its degree of roughness.
>
> The electronics group talked about "job security," "a small company," and "health and dental insurance." The shop floor production group talked about "more work," "upgrade of assembly," and "being in control of the job." [Discussion] themes in the shop floor production group were oriented toward people, growth in the division/company, and strategy. The inspection group mentioned an "expanded inspection department," "improvements in quality control," the "quality control system," or "partnership." Some [other discussion] themes in the group were growth of the division/company and orientation toward people.

In yet another study, Drake, Koch, and Steckler identified three types of occupational subcultures that exist in public sector organizations.[3] They identified the "bureaucrat subculture" as being composed of public servants who manage the day-to-day operations of public services and make decisions about the allocation of public resources. They contend that members of this subculture build and maintain systems of public service, with a focus on how operations can be made more efficient and how public resources can best be used. One of their primary functions is to enforce laws and regulations that reflect changing political preferences and biases.

These researchers characterize the "politician subculture" as being composed of appointed leaders who manage the political processes and tensions inherent in enacting directives from the three branches of government, managing on behalf of various interests and the public good, and providing leadership within their agencies. Members of this subculture are seen as operating at the level of policy, where advocacy, negotiation, and compromise are the primary processes by which public resources are allocated. The question of who benefits and who loses cannot be ignored within this occupational subculture.

Finally, these researchers identified what they call the "scientist" subculture, which links together scientists and other technical specialists in public organizations with other members of their worldwide occupational community and reference group. They argue that similar education, socialization, and training together with far-reaching labor markets enable members of this subculture to hold values, beliefs, and assumptions that often have more in common with fellow scientists around the world than with bureaucrats or politicians in the same agency.

The common link between occupational subcultures described in the foregoing sections is that they can be divided into two general categories: technical orientation and nontechnical orientation. In other words, whether they are private-sector or public-sector organizations, in those with multiple subunits/departments there are subgroups of employees who belong to either a technical-oriented subculture or a nontechnical-oriented subculture. This is especially true in the case of what we call "technology-intensive" organizations.

While not discounting other types of organizations, research suggests that more and more organizations are being classified as "technology-intensive" and are likely to have alignment problems with their technical and nontechnical subcultures. Therefore, throughout the remainder of this chapter, we will focus on "technology-intensive" organizations and the technical and nontechnical subcultures within them. We begin by defining "technology-intensive" organizations and then look at the differences between these two subcultures (and the characteristics of their members) that may cause them to be misaligned.

What Are Technology-Intensive Organizations?

Technology-intensive organizations can be distinguished from those that are not technology intensive by two key attributes: (1) the technological intensiveness of their strategies, and (2) the volatility of their environments. For example, technology-intensive organizations adopt technology-intensive strategies resulting in products like computers, telecommunication systems, electronics, and so on. These organizations are also subject to environmental volatility (for example, rapid changes and uncertainty) in both product/process technology and market demand. For the most part, then, when we refer to technology-intensive organizations we are referring to high-tech organizations such as IBM, Hewlett Packard, Sun Microsystems, Intel, Texas Instruments, AT&T, WorldCom, Sprint, and other similar organizations.

Technical and Nontechnical Workers

Technical occupations (for example, jobs in engineering, computers, electronics, information technology) are among the most rapidly growing in the U.S. economy. Employment in these occupations is projected to increase by 23.3 percent between 2002 and 2012.[4] Continuing demand for new computer applications, innovative products, new medical treatments, and so on, is largely responsible for growth in these occupational areas. However, growth in support occupations is also occurring at a rapid pace.[5] Growth in these nontechnical occupations (for example, marketing, finance, human resource management, and so on) reflects a need for technology-intensive organizations to ensure that their outputs are competitive in the marketplace.

The simultaneous growth in technical and nontechnical occupations within technology-intensive organizations raises an important issue. The issue arises from distinct differences in the career anchors (that is, patterns of self-perceived talents, motives, and values that serve to guide, constrain, stabilize, and integrate careers) of technical workers and nontechnical workers. For example, technical workers have a "technical competence" career anchor and are strongly inclined to exercise their technical talents.[6] It might be said that the effect of this career anchor on technical workers has been to transform them into "technologists" who have developed a culture that is uniquely theirs.[7]

Nontechnical workers, on the other hand, are more likely to have a "strategic competence" career anchor, where their inclination is to focus on teamwork and creating product-market synergy that affords their organization a competitive advantage in the marketplace.[8] It might be ar-

gued that the effect of this career anchor transforms nontechnical workers into "commercialists" who have developed a culture that is uniquely
theirs. Evidence in the management literature suggests that differences in
the career anchors of technical and nontechnical workers leads to the development of two separate subcultures within technology-intensive organizations. The issue raised, in light of this evidence, is whether the
subcultures created by these differences are aligned (or misaligned) such
that performance in technology-intensive organizations is optimized (or
suboptimized).

Academic research has shown that misaligned subcultures are most
likely to occur in technology-intensive organizations.[9] The reason is that
technology-intensive organizations are more likely to have several technical and nontechnical subunits (or departments). In addition to the nontechnical subunits (for example, marketing, human resource management,
manufacturing, and accounting), they also are likely to have several technical subunits (for example, engineering, research and development, information technology, computer technology, and technical support). In
organizations that are not very technology intensive (for example, finance,
transportation, health, retail sales), technical subunits are either small or
nonexistent. Subsequently, technical subcultures are not likely to evolve in
these organizations, and thus the type of subculture misalignment (that is,
technical and nontechnical) we refer to in this chapter is not likely to be
much of an issue.

In support of this rationale, there is evidence to suggest that corporate
culture may be stronger in organizations where there is a preponderance
of either technical subunits or a preponderance of nontechnical subunits,
but not several of both.[10] The rationale is that in organizations where
there are several of each type of subunit, departmentalizing technical and
nontechnical workers into separate subunits allows distinct subcultures to
evolve to the extent that a cultural misalignment between the two subcultures is created. The result is a fragmented and weak corporate culture,
which results in suboptimal or inferior organizational performance.

Technical and Nontechnical Subcultures

The message we have attempted to convey up to this point in our discussion is that technology-intensive organizations with several technical and

nontechnical subunits must be concerned with managing two distinct cultures: the "corporate economic" culture, which is subscribed to by nontechnical workers, and the "scientific-technical" culture, which is subscribed to by technical workers. A distinguishing characteristic of the technical subculture is that its members tend to gravitate toward occupational loyalty. That is, technical workers generally rate the recognition received from peers in their profession to be of greater importance than organizational recognition; they usually view the organization as a means or a vehicle to help them achieve their professional goals.[11]

A distinguishing characteristic of the nontechnical subculture, in contrast, is that its members are generally more oriented to the organization for which they work; recognition coming from the formal reward system within the organization is more important to them than occupational recognition. This distinguishing characteristic suggests that the values of nontechnical workers are quite different from those of technical workers: whereas the former conform to cultural norms that stress the organizational value system, the latter conform to cultural norms that stress freedom in pursuing professional goals, which may be due in part to the restrictions imposed on the latter's professional autonomy by organizational bureaucracy.[12]

Although they belong to a different subculture, both technical and nontechnical workers are important to organizational performance efforts. This is particularly true in technology-intensive organizations, where technical workers are their lifeblood, and the essential role of nontechnical workers is to ensure that the breakthroughs made by technical workers afford the technology-intensive organization a competitive advantage in the marketplace. It is clear, however, that these two subcultures must be aligned if this competitive advantage is to be achieved and sustained.

Aligned or Misaligned?

Up to this point in our discussion, we have provided conceptual and theoretical evidence that a misalignment is likely to exist between technical and nontechnical subcultures. Is there empirical evidence indicating that technical and nontechnical subcultures within technology-intensive organizations are likely to be misaligned? To answer this question, we conducted an empirical investigation to see whether differences exist in technical and nontechnical workers' level of commitment to the values of technology-intensive organizations. Based on our prior discussion of the relationship between values commitment and corporate culture, assessing the extent to which technical and nontechnical workers are committed to the values of the technology-intensive organizations for which they work should provide an accurate assessment of the extent to which these two subcultures are aligned or misaligned.

As part of our empirical investigation, we analyzed data collected from 1,729 technical workers (employed in the areas of research and development, information systems, information technology, and technology support) and 1,624 nontechnical workers (employed in the areas of customer service, finance, human resources, and marketing). The workers were employed by fifteen technology-intensive organizations (including computer hardware and software manufacturers and computer service providers) located in the Silicon Valley in northern California.[13] The workers' level of commitment to the values of their respective organizations was measured by asking them to respond to several statements on a five-point scale, ranging from strongly disagree (1 point) to strongly agree (5 points). The statements consisted of the following: 1. I take pride in working for this organization; 2. "I would recommend this organization to my friends as a good place to work; 3. "I would recommend that my friends buy stock in this organization"; and 4. "I would recommend this organization's products/services to my friends." The rationale behind these statements is that positive responses reflect workers' loyalty to the organizations and thus their commitment to the organizations' values.

Our analysis revealed that the average response to these statements for technical workers was 3.95 and the average response for nontechnical workers was 4.05. Results of a statistical analysis of these averages suggested that the higher average for nontechnical workers meant that they were more committed to the technology-intensive organizations we studied than were the technical workers working for these organizations. Based on our statistical analysis, which indicated statistical significance, we concluded that the technical and nontechnical subcultures in these firms were misaligned.

Misalignment Determinants

What causes the misalignment between technical and nontechnical subcultures in technology-intensive organizations? The literature we consulted suggests that the misalignment might be traced to technical and nontechnical workers' dominant emphases within organizations. For instance, it has been argued that nontechnical workers are imbued with a "strategic orientation," where the importance of the relationship between the organization and its external environment is clearly understood, and that technical workers are imbued with a "technical orientation."[14] Technical workers' orientation is argued to produce a singular emphasis on costs, which ignores the customer, and a scientific-technical point of view that values tools, equipment, and gadgets over markets and service.[15]

It has also been argued that the technical orientation characteristic of the technical subculture is largely a result of the narrow, task-oriented perspective that is often adopted by technical workers. Although this perspective might be partly attributed to their technical training, the type of jobs they are usually assigned to, which typically give them responsibility for only a small part of organizational processes and activities, may contribute significantly to their adoption of such a perspective. Nontechnical workers, because of their strategic orientation, are usually cross-trained in several areas of the organization and thus are exposed to various organizational processes and activities. However, due to technical workers' "quasi-isolation," they gain a severely limited sense of market needs and corporate competitive strategy.[16]

The inherent values subscribed to by individuals imbued with a strategic orientation (nontechnical workers) are clearly different from those subscribed to by individuals imbued with a technical orientation (technical workers); this difference provides insights into why the technical subculture can be, and frequently is, out of alignment with the nontechnical subculture in technology-intensive organizations. The misalignment between technical and nontechnical subcultures can hold important implications for strategy within technology-intensive organizations. What are some of these implications?

Strategy Implications

A management concern within technology-intensive organizations might involve determining the pros and cons associated with maintaining the two distinct subcultures versus bringing them into alignment. We contend that the strategic benefits of bringing the two subcultures into alignment outweigh any advantages of maintaining the two distinct subcultures. For example, it has been suggested that the technical subculture must be aligned (to a large degree) with the nontechnical subculture if management expects investments in resources that support organization strategy to pay off.[17] It has also been suggested that corporate culture can either be a strategic tool or a strategic constraint, depending on the degree to which subcultures within organizations are in alignment.[18]

The rationale is that a strong corporate culture, where subcultures are in precise alignment, affects not only the process of strategy formulation but also sets a performance tone for making the strategy effective once it is implemented.[19] In such organizations, employees in all subunits know and support the organization's mission, objectives, and strategies, and organizational performance is enhanced. In organizations with a weak corporate culture, where subcultures are misaligned, no clear sense of purpose exists.[20] Consequently, a reduction in organizational performance is likely to ensue.

The strategy implications of aligning the technical and nontechnical subcultures are particularly evident in the policies that are related to the decisions emanating from the organizations' technical and nontechnical subunits. For example, decisions emanating from nontechnical subunits are almost always sent up for review by higher-level managers. However, the operating decisions made within technical subunits are seldom subjected to review by top management. As a result, the organization may, over time, become (in effect) captive to a series of decisions made almost autonomously by a variety of technical workers who, through no fault of their own, are absorbed in their own professional interests and crafts.[21] Each of these decisions may appear to be small and nonstrategic in its individual impact, yet together they may have a significant impact on the organization's overall strategy. Whether the nature of this impact is supportive or nonsupportive of overall strategy depends on the degree to which the technical subculture is aligned with the nontechnical subculture within technology-intensive organizations.

Performance Implications

The model we presented in Chapter 1 (Figure 1.1) suggested that the alignment of technical and nontechnical subcultures results in superior organizational performance and the misalignment of these subcultures results in inferior organizational performance. Just what do we mean by organizational performance? A general measure of performance, the one we adopt in this book, is how well an organization achieves its goals.[22] Of course organizations can have multiple goals, in which the achievement of some can be suboptimal without having significant implications for the organization. However, suboptimal achievement of some goals can have a deleterious impact on an organization. Two examples illustrate both of these cases when there is misalignment between technical and nontechnical subcultures in organizations.

The first example is taken from a study where the focus was on a group of employees working in a research and development subunit (technical subculture) within a technology-intensive organization and a group of employees working in the marketing department (nontechnical subculture) in the same organization.[23] This particular study involved assessing the effectiveness of these two subcultures as they worked together to meet the technical and functional requirements of the company's customers (the goal). The results of this study suggested that because the two subcultures were not aligned, in terms of sharing common values, beliefs, and expectations of how to go about achieving the goal, difficulties arose in the two groups' ability to successfully meet customer requirements. Although there were no serious consequences from the failure of the two groups to achieve the goal standard, organizational performance was suboptimal (or inferior) in terms of achieving this particular goal.

The second example comes from a study of the January 28, 1986, space shuttle *Challenger* disaster, where the space orbiter and its seven-member crew were lost 73 seconds after launch when a booster failure resulted in the breakup of the vehicle. The study attributes the disaster to (1) differing perceptions and priorities of the engineers (technical subculture) and management (nontechnical subculture) at Thiokol (the technology-intensive organization), (2) a preoccupation with roles and role responsibilities on the part of engineers and managers, (3) contrasting corporate cultures at Thiokol and its parent company, Morton, and (4) a failure both by engineers and managers to exercise individual and moral responsibility.

This example highlights how the "technical competence" career anchor of technical workers and the "strategic competence" career anchor of nontechnical workers can be very different, and how the difference between them can indicate the existence of a fragmented corporate culture within the same organization. Whereas the strategic competence of managers in the organization led them to be concerned with the goals of on-time performance, adhering to the requirements contained within the contract, and public relations, the technical competence of engineers in the organization led them to be concerned with the goals of eliminating the design and reliability shortcomings of the o-ring sealing mechanisms (which were linked directly to the explosion of the *Challenger*) used on the booster rockets.

The *Challenger* disaster is an extreme case where a misalignment of technical and nontechnical subcultures may not only result in inferior organizational performance but have irrevocable consequences for an organization. Although the consequences for the organization in the first example were not as serious as the consequences for the Thiokol organization in the second example, both serve to point out the implications that a misalignment of technical and nontechnical subcultures can have for organizational performance. These examples also point out a need for management of technology-intensive organizations to ensure that these two subcultures are in alignment.

Chapter Summary and Conclusions

A prerequisite for aligning technical and nontechnical subcultures is to make sure technical and nontechnical workers are committed to the dominant values of technology-intensive organizations. In every organization there are certain core values that guide strategic focus and contribute to the success of organization strategy and performance. In order to promote the successful alignment of technical and nontechnical subcultures within technology-intensive organizations, managers of these organizations must first identify these core values and then make sure they are clearly understood and accepted by both technical and nontechnical workers.

Ethnic and Racial Subcultures

Results of a recent Census Bureau Current Population Survey indicate that 33.1 million immigrants (legal and illegal), from different ethnic and cultural backgrounds, currently live in the United States. Selected highlights of the survey include the following:

- More than 3.3 million legal and illegal immigrants have entered the United States since January of 2000.
- The number of immigrants living in the United States is unprecedented.
- Immigrants account for 11.5 percent of the total population of the United States, the highest percentage in seventy years.
- Immigration has become the determinant factor in population growth, adding more than 2 million people to the United States population each year and accounting for at least two-thirds of U.S. population growth.
- Immigrants now constitute 14.6 percent of the U.S. workforce. If immigration remains high, this percentage could double by 2050.

The information provided in Table 5.1 indicates the areas of the world where immigrants are coming from. Whereas most of those immigrating

TABLE 5.1   Immigration Changes in the United States

Region	1901–1910 %	1991–2003 %
Europe	92.6	15.2
Asia	3.4	31.3
Canada	1.9	2.3
Mexico	0.5	24.6
Caribbean	0.1	6.2
Central America	0.1	6.2
South America	0.2	6.2
Africa	0.1	4.3

to the United States in the early twentieth century were from Europe, the majority of the immigrants currently being admitted are from Asia, Caribbean island nations, Mexico, and Central and South America. The information provided in Table 5.2 shows the top twenty countries of origin for those immigrating to the United States, for fiscal year 2002. The information provided in these two tables reveals the extent and significance of immigration in the United States.

The map provided in Figure 5.1 shows where immigrants entering the United States are settling. Most states are experiencing moderate to high immigration growth. Moreover, since many of these immigrants become immediate participants in the U.S. workforce, organizations conducting business in these states can expect an increase in the number of immigrants in their respective workforces. The result is a cultur-

TABLE 5.2   Top Countries of Origin for U.S. Immigrants

Mexico	20.6	Korea	2.0
India	6.7	Russia	2.0
China	5.8	Haiti	1.9
Philippines	4.8	Canada	1.8
Vietnam	3.2	Colombia	1.8
El Salvador	2.9	Guatemala	1.5
Cuba	2.7	United Kingdom	1.5
Bosnia-Herzegovina	2.4	Jamaica	1.4
Dominican Republic	2.1	Pakistan	1.3
Ukraine	2.0	Iran	1.2

ally diverse workplace in terms of culture, race, and ethnicity, as well as a host of diverse value systems.

International Value Systems

Given these trends in immigration, managers of U.S. organizations can expect a plethora of divergent value systems to permeate their collective workplaces. A significant concern of organization management is how to align the values of these international subcultures with the values that define their corporate culture. In the next few sections of this chapter we examine the value systems of what are called cultural clusters.[1] Specifically, we examine Asian, Latin American, and European clusters. As indicated in

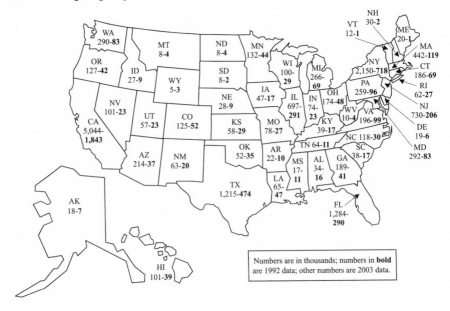

FIGURE 5.1   Where Immigrants Are Settling

Table 5.1 and Table 5.2, these areas represent the greatest proportion of the culturally diverse groups immigrating to the United States. In addition to discussing the value systems of these cultural clusters, the value systems of the Japanese, East Indian, and Australian cultures is discussed as well. Some unique aspects of these cultures warrant their inclusion in discussions of diverse cultural values.

Value System of the Asian Cultural Cluster

The Koreans, Japanese, and Chinese have distinct cultures.[2] However, they are connected by a common social philosophy stretching back many centuries. In fact, this social philosophy has spread across Asia, extending to Indonesia, Malaysia, India, Taiwan, the Philippines, Thailand, and other Asian countries where intercultural migration has occurred. A common thread woven through these Asian cultures is the strong influence of their dominant religions such as Confucianism, Taoism, and others in the countries of Chinese descent, and in Japan, Buddhism and Shintoism. A value stressed by these religions is social interaction, which is the basis of the strong group identification, formality and courtesy, modesty, humility, and taciturn demeanor for which Asian cultures are known.

In Asian organizations, the prevailing values espoused by corporate culture are loyalty, accommodation, and honoring authority. For example, the founder of Korea's largest family-run conglomerate, Samsung, wrote an employee policy in 1938 stating that loyalty to the organization would be highly valued in all employees. Similar policies exist in most Asian organizations. Through accommodation, Asian employees seek to minimize dissent. Accommodation ensures that confrontations are avoided; statements are carefully worded to avoid hurting the feelings of others. The values of loyalty and accommodation exist in the shadow of honoring authority. That is, most Asian organizations are very hierarchical, and authority is clearly defined and defended. Consequently, subordinates are very careful not to offend individuals who are older in age or in positions of higher authority. These corporate culture values, which exist in most Asian organizations, are part of the larger value system of many Asian cultures.

The Japanese Value System

Although there are some commonalities, the underlying cultural values subscribed to by the Japanese are not found in other Asian cultures.[3] As in other cultures, Japan's religious teachings have had a great influence on the development of its value system. For example, the Confucian influence can be observed in their emphasis on hierarchy and position, while the subtle and indirect demeanor and hidden meaning in the Japanese disposition can be traced to Zen Buddhism. A key aspect of the Japanese value system is that they view themselves as members of a group first, and then as an individual. Part of the group identification involves a deeply rooted interdependence among group members and tacit obligations to the group. One is expected to get along in a group environment, to adhere to the established formalities, respecting the clear class distinctions, and to behave in a conventional, predictable manner. In general, the qualities of sameness, evenness, and consistency of values and behavior dominate the cultural value system of Japanese society.

Elements of this value system are reflected in the corporate culture of Japanese organizations. This pervasive corporate culture fosters norms that focus on courtesy, conformity, and caring for others within the organization. Deference based on age, rank, role, and gender are among the required behaviors of all employees. Harmony is of paramount importance. However, the suppression of women in corporate settings is a major factor that characterizes the value system of Japanese organizations. For example, Yuko Ogasawara found that in Japanese companies with 100 or more employees, women make up only 1% of the total number of general managers, 3% of section managers, and 7% of subsection heads.[4]

Evidently, this value is portable. For example, the Japanese Ministry of Labor reported that 57 percent of the 331 Japanese corporations in the United States are concerned about being the target of an employment discrimination suit. Many of these suits are based on complaints by women who feel they are not receiving the promotions they deserve. The National Organization for Women (NOW) cited Mitsubishi as having a particularly poor record, stating that the company's insensitive response to complaints of sexual discrimination is an indication that there is still a long way to go before Japan's corporate culture really opens up to women.

In general, formality, loyalty, and predictability are important attributes of the corporate value system of Japanese organizations.

The East Indian Value System

In addition to various tribal groups, India has a large number of ethnic communities, including Bengalis, Gujaritis, Sikhs, and Muslims.[5] Each community has its own language, culture, and religion. The dominant religion is Hinduism, but there are substantial minority religions such as Islam, Sikhism, Jainism, Buddhism, Christianity, and Judaism. One indication of India's value system is that rather than attempting to assimilate these different cultures, customs, beliefs, languages, and religions into a unified whole, they are accepted as they are. Despite the disparity among the culture and value systems in India, the Asian influence is apparent in the common value of respect for age and position. Also included among the values of the middle class are a respect for education and competitive excellence. One of the most well-known aspects of India's cultural values is the caste system, which prescribes social status at birth and offers no opportunity for upward mobility.

In East Indian organizations, perspectives toward work are more relaxed than in many other cultures. For example, appointment schedules are not strictly adhered to. However, protocol is an important value, and formal titles and names are almost always used, even among friends. In terms of managerial values, Indian managers at upper levels of the organization tend to underplay the use of power and are inclined to use consultative and participatory styles of management. At lower levels, however, managerial leadership tends to be paternalistic and autocratic, and power sharing with subordinates and workers is viewed as a weakness.

Value System of the Latin American Cultural Cluster

Even though they may come from a variety of countries (Mexico, South America, Central America, and the Caribbean), individuals from these Latin American cultures are drawn together by their common Spanish ancestry.[6] The religion of these countries is almost exclusively Roman Catholicism, which plays a central role in their overlapping value systems. A shared value in this system is strong family orientation. Family is a priority, and family obligations supersede business commitments. In most Latin American cultures, men are considered superior to women. Nevertheless, women and the elderly are highly respected.

Marriage and education are also shared values in Latin American cultures and are the two primary vehicles for mobility, as in many other cultures. However, social interaction among classes, which fosters an aspiration to excel in education and offers opportunities for marrying outside one's circle, is distinctly limited. As a general rule, education, manners, and land ownership are important indicators of one's social position. Social position is extremely important in Latin American cultures.

In Latin American organizations, the value system emphasizes status and rank. Managers generally do not socialize with subordinates. However, managers are often considered to be a part of the workers' extended family—a role that can be characterized as patronizing. Consequently, loyalty is an important aspect of the personal bond between manager and subordinate. Because of the respect for managerial authority, a participative management style is not prevalent in Latin organizations; such a style would make Latin American workers feel uncomfortable.

Moreover, employees do not initiate tasks on their own; they are expected to take direction from managers out of respect for authority. Formality is important, but time conventions and perspectives on work are very relaxed in organizations. The practice of handing out "gratuities" or bribes for getting something accomplished has long been an expected form of conducting business in Latin American organizations. However, in recent years, reforms have been instituted to more closely align business practices with those of U.S. organizations. The practice of nepotism is also well established in Latin American organizations and is not considered unethical behavior.

Value System of the Eastern European Cultural Cluster

Because of the political-economic influence of Russia in this region, we will consider the republics of the former Soviet Union (Russia, Ukraine, Georgia, and so on) and its satellite countries (Poland, Hungary, Bulgaria, Czechoslovakia, and so on) as constituting this cultural cluster.[7] Over one hundred ethnic groups make up this cluster, but they can be classified into five major groups: Slavs, Baltic peoples, people of the Caucasus, people of Soviet Central Asia, and mixed. Unlike most other cultures, religion plays a relatively minor role in determining the values of groups and individuals making up this cultural cluster.

Since the breakup of the Soviet Union, the countries constituting this cluster have undergone significant economic and political change; many are still in transition. Observers of business practices in this cluster have noted that economic and political volatility, combined with years of suppressing the development of organizations, has resulted in an Eastern European corporate value system that is significantly different than that found in organizations of Western cultures, to the extent that it may be difficult for many Western managers to comprehend. The shortcoming in the system appears to be top management's inability to adopt and conform to corporate values.

Value System of the Western European Cultural Cluster

Several countries make up this large cultural group, and many subscribe to similar cultural values. For simplicity's sake, only France and Great Britain will be considered in this section.[8] As a matter of general protocol, individuals in Western Europe tend to be rather formal and conservative. First names are never used without invitation, and that usually comes only after long association. Moreover, individuals with academic titles and degrees expect them to be used by those addressing them. And, like many other cultures, punctuality is a sign of courtesy.

Generally, the religious culture of both France and Great Britain is predominantly Christian: France is primarily Roman Catholic, and Great Britain is primarily Anglican. Despite some subtle differences in their value systems, there are many commonalities. Both share a respect for discipline and responsibility, a low tolerance for ambiguity, a view of oneself as an individual first and then as a member of a larger group, high mobility (both socially and occupationally), and esteem for education. Some differences in their value systems stem from differences in ethnic makeup.

The ethnic population of France is a blend of Celtic, Teutonic, and Latin and includes a mixture of Nordic, Alpine, Mediterranean, and a large minority of North African Arabs and a small group of blacks from former French colonies. Because of the diverse ethnic population, most French people consider themselves members of their family first, then citizens of France, and then members of organizations. As part of greater French society, they share in a French culture that is well known for its flair for the arts and the joy of living. Another shared value common to France's diverse culture is the emphasis on tradition and *comme il faut*, or the way things are done. The concept of success is another value that is prominent in French culture. Success is generally judged by a person's educational level, family background, and financial status rather than one's personal accomplishments.

The overwhelming majority of the ethnic composition of Great Britain is English, Scottish, Irish, and Welsh, with sizable minorities of West Indians, East Indians, and Pakistanis. Despite the diversity of cultures, a basic sense of fair play underlies Great Britain's value system. Status is critical, and tradition and subtlety are key personal characteristics that are important in establishing one's status in society. Although the British often appear to be aloof, their demeanor is more a reflection of personal privacy and modesty, along with a tendency not to register emotion in public. Generally speaking, the melding of democratic principles with a highly visible and much loved monarchy has led to a culture that is very formal and conservative, yet one that values personal space and independence.

In European organizations, a strong concept of social order and an emphasis on rules exemplify the corporate value system. Management is formal and hierarchical, with decision-making authority concentrated at the top levels of the organization. However, many of the younger managers are moving away from the formal and hierarchical corporate values to something closer to the informal and ostensible egalitarianism more typical of the corporate value system found in U.S. organizations.

The Australian Value System

Because of its origin as a British penal colony, British cultural values are reflected in Australia's value system.[9] A marked departure from British values is reflected in Australians' distrust of authority and rules. The Australian saying, "Cutting down tall poppies to size," typifies their penchant for being self-reliant and reflects their disdain for status based on social class and wealth. Australians also tend to eschew formality, both in social custom and in the use of titles, preferring to use first names quickly after initial introductions and formalities are over. Similar to Great Britain, a deeply ingrained sense of fair play and merit-based esteem underlie the value system of Australia. Despite this adherence to fair play, racial and gender discrimination are rather strong. Australia is still a male-dominated, machismo society, and immigration, especially from Asian countries, is severely restricted.

Considering their informal nature and de-emphasis on money, Australian organizations are very competitive. Making profits is the paramount objective, and Australians have little sympathy for failure. Paradoxically, Australian workers express admiration for "bludgers"— those employees who appear to be very productive but are in reality producing very little. Excessive courtesy and protocol in organizational settings are considered to be a waste of time, and friendships are not allowed to interfere with work responsibilities. Generally, the prevailing corporate value in Australian organizations is reflected in the theme, "It is not how one wins, but that one wins is what matters."

American Value Systems

Like Anglo-Australians, Anglo-Americans in the United States share a common language and cultural heritage with Anglo-Europeans in Great Britain.[10] However, many would argue that differences between Anglo-American culture and other cultures are vast. For example, Anglo-Americans are often viewed by members of other cultures as being very informal, direct, competitive, punctual, and obsessed with cleanliness and as being achievers and questioners.

Generally, though, Anglo-Americans view themselves as being caring and generous people who value their independence and entrepreneurial spirit. Most Anglo-Americans, like Anglo-Europeans in Great Britain, also view themselves first as individuals and then as a member of a larger group. And, similar to Anglo-Europeans in Great Britain, a basic sense of fair play underlies the value system of Anglo-Americans.

This sense of fair play also extends to the many ethnic cultures coexisting in the United States. This particular cultural value is reflected in the term often used to describe the United States, the American "melting pot," which conveys equal opportunity for all who wish to participate in the American system.

Values of American Ethnic Subcultures

In addition to immigrants, ethnic minorities (including Hispanic Americans, Asian Americans, Native Americans, and African Americans) are contributing to significant population growth in the United States. According to 2004 U.S. Census Bureau statistics, Hispanic Americans, who represented 12.6 percent of the U.S. population in 2000, are projected to represent 24.4 percent by the year 2050. African Americans represented 12.7 percent of the U.S. population in 2000, and are projected to represent 14.6 percent by the year 2050. Asian Americans represented 3.8 percent of the U.S. population in 2000, and are projected to represent 8 percent by the year 2050. Finally, other non-white ethnic groups (e.g., Native Americans, Alaska Natives, Native Hawaiian and other Pacific Islanders) represented 2.5 percent of the U.S. population in 2000 and are projected to represent 5.3 percent by the year 2050.[11]

According to the Bureau of Labor Statistics, ethnic minorities are also expected to enter the U.S. workforce in record numbers between now and the year 2010. For example, African Americans represented 10.8 percent of the U.S. workforce in 2003; Hispanic Americans represented 7.7 percent; and Asian Americans represented 6.0 percent. It is estimated that in 2010 there will be a 20.7 percent increase in the number of African Americans participating in the workforce, a 36.3 percent increase in the number of Hispanic Americans participating in the workforce, and a 44.1 percent increase in the number of Asian Americans participating in the workforce.

It has been suggested that the various ethnic subcultures of the United States embrace distinct values. These are summarized as follows:

- *Anglo-American values:* individualistic, direct, extroverted, spontaneous, casual, egalitarian, informal, rational communication.
- *African American values:* camaraderie and connection with heritage, direct, informal, emotional expressiveness, strong community or church ties, stylized communication.
- *Asian American Values:* other-oriented, group before self, self-controlled, disciplined, reserved, defined roles, indirect communication.
- *Hispanic American values:* relationships are priority, well-defined gender roles, loyal, expressive, spontaneous, physical closeness, courteous communication.
- *Native American values:* oneness of all, holistic orientation, extended family, community-oriented, privacy, noninterference, reserved communication.

The value differences among these domestic subcultures suggests the concept of "ethnic culture," which can be described as the component of ethnicity that refers to that pattern of behaviors and beliefs that sets a cultural group apart from others. For ethnic minorities (African Americans, Asian Americans, Hispanic Americans, Native Americans), the pattern of cultural difference is more a product of the American experience than anything else. Unlike other ethnic minorities, Hispanic Americans tend to describe the pattern of cultural differences in terms of behavioral styles, emotional expression, and personal values. With respect to values, they express an appreciation for the Hispanic American emphasis on discipline and instilling in their children a strict sense of morality. In general, Hispanic Americans believe that they are more respectful and generally have "better values" than those subscribed to by mainstream America.

Members of ethnic subcultures may adapt to cultural differences in two distinctly different ways. *Assimilation* is the process by which members of ethnic groups adapt their behavioral patterns and norms to those of the dominant culture. With respect to ethnic minorities in the United States, many adapt to the norms and values subscribed to by mainstream America. In doing so, however, some may camouflage their true feelings and/or suppress aspects of their own culture in public or in the presence of members of the dominant culture. *Deculturation* is the alternative scenario, in which members of ethnic subcultures retain their distinct set of norms and values with no attempt to integrate or synthesize the value system of the dominant culture.

A classic example of deculturation is the existence of "Chinatowns" in many major American cities, where there is minimal interaction between the residents of Chinatown and those outside of that community. Another example is the position of African Americans who are especially sensitive to "the sacred closet of race." Often raised to conceal their cultural experience from outsiders, African Americans may label as "traitors" those who reveal to members of the dominant culture their intimate feelings and experiences. As a result, many African Americans have been taught to isolate themselves and to mistrust those who subscribe to dominant culture values.

Aligning Ethnic Subcultures

In 1990, AT&T implemented a program of corporate culture change. During the change process, top management at AT&T explicitly articulated the organization's value system to employees. Training was given to employees to reshape their norms and modify their behavior in support of the organization's corporate values. As a means of maintaining the integrity of the corporate culture change, recruitment efforts targeted only those potential employees whose personal values were consistent with AT&T's value system.[12]

If AT&T were making this corporate culture change in 2005, would AT&T's recruitment efforts be successful? In other words, would the company be able to find, from among a highly culturally diverse labor pool, enough recruits whose values were consistent with their corporate value system? How would these new recruits fit into AT&T's corporate culture? Let's draw from assimilationist theory for a possible answer to this question. From a societal perspective, classical assimilationist theory suggests that newcomers to a given society choose among three nonexclusive options:

1. Assimilate the mainstream's cultural values
2. Assimilate a particular minority's or subculture's values
3. Preserve their own cultural values

One study found evidence in support of this theory. In response to a survey, 48 percent of the Vietnamese responding considered themselves "Vietnamese," as opposed to "Vietnamese American," "Asian," or "American" (option 3). In contrast, 48 percent of the Haitians responding to the same survey considered themselves "Haitian Americans" (option 1), and 42 percent of the Nicaraguans responding to the survey considered themselves to be "Latino" or "Hispanic" (option 2).[13]

Within the context of organizations, the results of this survey suggest that an issue to consider is whether corporate culture erases or at least diminishes national or societal cultural characteristics or whether a racially and ethnically diverse workforce leads to misalignments in corporate culture. According to a classic 1983 study conducted by Andre Laurent, the latter issue is likely to be the case.[14] Laurent's research revealed that employees bring their race, ethnicity, and cultural values to the workplace.

This researchers contends that many managers assume that employees working for the same organization, even if they are from different racial, ethnic, and cultural backgrounds, are more similar than different. In reality,

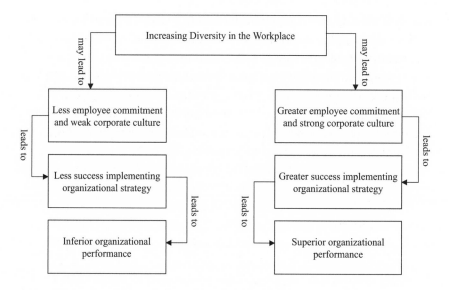

FIGURE 5.2   Diversity and Organizational Performance

however, employees adopt what has been called reactive ethnic identity. That is, according to Laurent, they maintain and even strengthen their racial, ethnic, and cultural differences in organizations. Moreover, Laurent's research concluded that although organizations may be becoming more similar, people within organizations strive to maintain their racial, ethnic, and cultural uniqueness.

Chapter Summary and Conclusions

Census data indicate that culturally diverse groups will make up an increasingly large proportion of the workforce of U.S. organizations in the future. Cultural theorists have suggested that these various subcultures have distinctly different values and norms, which may significantly influence employee behavior in organizations.[15]

As these culturally diverse groups increasingly become participants in U.S. organizations, the corporate cultures of these organizations may be affected. As illustrated in Figure 5.2, increasing racial, ethnic, and cultural diversity in the workplace may lead to less employee commitment. The rationale for this scenario is that the misalignment of the different value systems that employees bring to the workplace will result in a decrease in the overall commitment levels within the organization.

Alternatively, if an organization is able to successfully manage employees' different value systems, greater employee commitment will result. Employee commitment is a critically important factor because it affects corporate culture, which in turn affects strategy implementation and, most importantly, organizational performance.

Gender and Generational Subcultures

According to the U.S. Department of Labor, women comprised 47 percent of the total labor force in 2003 and 59.5 percent of women age 16 and over were working or looking for work in 2003. In a 2004 report by Mitra Toossi, the percentage of women in the labor force will increase from 46.5 to 47.5 percent between 2002 and 2012.[1] Moreover, this report indicated that the participation rate of women in the labor force was 52.6 percent in 1982, 57.8 percent in 1992, 59.6 percent in 2002, and is projected to increase to 61.6 percent in 2012. As a group, women represent the highest percentage of new entrants to the U.S. labor force and are expected to dominate the workplace in the twenty-first century.[2]

Physiognomically, the typical new entrant to the U.S. workforce is expected to be a mature woman, probably an immigrant, whose first language is not English.[3] Language notwithstanding, it has been argued that as organizations place greater emphasis on teamwork and management by consensus, there will inevitably be a move toward hiring more women into management and technical occupations traditionally dominated by men. Moreover, since women represent a high and growing proportion of those students graduating with business and technical degrees, it is likely that the number of women in managerial and technical jobs, in domestic as well as international organizations, will increase.[4]

Gender Differences in the Workplace

When gender subcultures are considered, the increasing proportion of women in the workforce has implications for corporate culture, in that men and women think differently about their work. Indeed, research has shown that employees and managers have different expectations in the workplace, based on their national backgrounds and socialization.[5] This is equally true for gender subcultures. For example, women are generally more hesitant and less forceful than men in expressing their ideas in the workplace because they have been socialized since childhood to avoid boastful or aggressive behavior.[6]

In other research related to perceptions of what traits were desirable in the workplace, it was established that male managers considered the following traits to be most appropriate: outspokenness, forcefulness, and ability to command respect and to ensure one is listened to.[7] So-called feminine traits, such as use of emotion, intuition, and consultation, were not regarded as appropriate workplace traits. Although the author of this study asserts that the attribution of these different traits to men and to women may be based on perceptions and preconceived ideas rather than realities, the implications are that gender subcultures in the workplace are not in precise alignment.

From an international perspective, a Hong Kong study of male and female communication styles in the workplace found little difference between males and females in three categories of communication: encouraging, acknowledging, and discouraging.[8] However, men tended to be more encouraging toward other men than toward women. Women also tended to express more encouragement toward men than toward women. This was in contrast to American studies that have shown that men are more encouraging toward men, and women are more encouraging toward women.

Other research has focused on gender differences with respect to perceptions of self-confidence and self-assessment of ability. For example, researchers have found that girls and women tend to underestimate or undervalue their own capabilities, whereas boys and men tend to overestimate theirs.[9] For the most part, this research suggests that girls believe they have to be better than average to succeed in male-dominated fields. Still other research suggests that female senior managers tend to believe they have to be as well qualified as male managers, and in some cases more qualified, more ambitious, and more mobile than male managers.[10]

It has been suggested that the tendency to underestimate their own ability is also evident in the self-perceptions of women in technical occupations.[11] For example, in a study of gender issues in technical occupations, 70 percent of the male participants thought their technical ability was above average, compared with 52 percent of the female participants. Of male participants 18 percent considered their ability to be average, in comparison with 24 percent of the female participants.

The authors of the study noted that the female participants evidenced a relatively great need for support, which stemmed from two sources. First, the authors noted that more female than male participants reported that they had encountered obstacles on their career paths. Second, the female participants seemed more dependent on social support systems in overcoming obstacles. Other studies have confirmed that women are socialized to rely on supportive interaction.[12]

At the managerial level and from an international perspective, 42 of the 50 participants in one study of international female managers said their management behavior was questioned more frequently by colleagues and superiors than that of male managers.[13] This response was attributed to the fact that female managers were rare and therefore had higher visibility. The majority of the female managers in this study reported that they had adopted their own individualistic style of management, rather than conforming to either a "male" or a "female" model. However, the author of the study concluded that the research findings confirm that in male-dominated organizations, where promotions have largely been reserved for men, women are encouraged to enact gender roles that suit men's preferences, thereby reinforcing men's power and dominance.

Gender Interactions in the Workplace

In addition to gender differences in the workplace, research has shown that gender segregation is prominent in interaction patterns within different jobs and professions.[14] Related research suggests that this segregation first becomes noticeable in places like graduate school, where women begin to be excluded from casual, work-related discussions either because they take place in all-male environments, such as a locker room after a game of squash, or at times when women find it difficult to participate.[15]

In one study, for example, it was found that 54 percent of the female participants, as opposed to 40 percent of the male participants, thought they had sometimes interacted differently with male and female co-workers. Many of the female participants thought that their career advancement was impeded because they were unable to interact casually with their male co-workers, either because they were excluded from casual male groups or because it was difficult for them to interact comfortably with male co-workers in certain types of social settings.[16]

With respect to gender segregation in technical occupations, one study revealed that 40 percent of the female participants responded that they sometimes had difficulty interacting with their male co-workers and 25 percent thought that this was due to gender-based reasons.[17] The study found this to be especially true for women who had been employed in their organizations for more than four years. However, a study of male and female employees in an advertising company found that women tended to seek different networks for different purposes: male-dominated networks for career advancement purposes and female-dominated networks for friendship and support.

Gender Values Differences

Based on the results of a study on gender values, it was concluded that the values and interests of females collectively are different in important, measurable ways from those of males in American society.[18] According to the author of this study, these differences stem from the fact that men and women are socialized differently into two distinct cultures: manhood and womanhood. The author further concluded that although considerable geographic, generational, economic, religious, and ethnic variations exist, there is a constellation of gender-specific values.

Differences between the values held by males and females have been the subject of numerous studies. Typical of such studies is one that looked at value differences between males and females in the medical profession.

The authors of this study argued that whereas women tend to value patient care and teaching, elements that contribute to a medical school's local mission, men are more likely to value accomplishments such as national visibility, leadership, and scholarship, elements that contribute to their career goals.[19] While studies such as this derive differences in gender values from anecdotal evidence, a recent study derived differences from empirical analyses.[20]

In this study, the authors used a typology of personal values. This typology was developed into a value survey, which classified values into two distinct categories that represented rank-ordered human values.[21] The two categories were called "instrumental" values and "terminal" values. The instrumental values are the means by which behavior is guided toward the ultimate goals or end-states. These end-states are the terminal values. Instrumental values were further subdivided into two categories: moral instrumental values and competence instrumental values.

Moral instrumental values focus on using moral behavior to obtain goals and include values such as being broadminded, forgiving, helpful, honest, loving, loyal, obedient, polite, and responsible. Competence instrumental values focus on using competent behavior to obtain desired goals and include values such as being ambitious, capable, clean, courageous, imaginative, independent, intellectual, logical, and self-controlled.

Terminal values were also further subdivided into two categories: social terminal values and personal terminal values. Social terminal values focus on individual concerns with a world of peace, a world of beauty, equality, family security, freedom, mature love, national security, social recognition, and true friendship. Personal terminal values focus on the needs of self, which include a comfortable life, an exciting life, a sense of accomplishment, health, inner harmony, pleasure, salvation, self-respect, and wisdom.

The authors surveyed a group of males and a group of females for their study. The members of the two groups were asked to rank each of the values in order of importance. For each of the subcategories, they assigned a 1 to the most important value and a 9 to the least important value. The authors then used a statistical technique to determine the significance of differences between males and females on each of the values. The results are shown in Tables 6.1, 6.2, 6.3, and 6.4. The check marks in

TABLE 6.1   Social Terminal Value Rankings by Gender

Values	Females	Males	Difference?*
Family security	1	1	
True friendship	2	4	
Mature love	3	3	
Freedom	4	2	
Equality	5	5	
A world at peace	6	8	✓
Social recognition	7	7	
National security	8	6	
A world of beauty	9	9	

Source: Adapted from D. E. Giacomino and T. V. Eaton, "Personal values of accounting alumni: An empirical examination of differences by gender and age." *Journal of Managerial Issues* 15 (2003): 369–380.

* ✓ = significant gender difference on these particular values

the tables indicate which of the values are significantly different between the two groups.

An interesting and relevant finding of this study is that the female participants placed more importance on the values of helpful and loving (see Table 6.3). This suggests that females subscribe to a value system that focuses more on serving others. In contrast, the fact that the male participants gave high priority to the values of courageous, self-controlled, and imaginative (see Table 6.4) suggests that they are more self-oriented than the female participants. Overall, these differences indicate that there are likely to be important value misalignments between gender subcultures within organizations.

TABLE 6.2   Personal Terminal Value Rankings by Gender

Values	Females	Males	Difference?*
Health	1	1	
Self-respect	2	2	
Inner harmony	3	4	
Sense of accomplishment	4	5	
Salvation	5	3	
A comfortable life	6	8	
Wisdom	7	6	✓
Pleasure	8	9	✓
An exciting life	9	7	✓

SOURCE: Adapted from D. E. Giacomino and T. V. Eaton, "Personal values of accounting alumni: An empirical examination of differences by gender and age." *Journal of Managerial Issues* 15 (2003): 369–380.

* ✓ = significant gender difference on these particular values

Generational Types

With respect to having a potential impact on corporate culture alignment or misalignment, three generational subcultures are relevant. The first generational subculture is the "Baby Boomers." Based on government age classifications, these individuals were born between 1946 and 1964, and they number approximately 74 million people.[22] Approximately 50 percent of all U.S. workers are Baby Boomers.[23] The second generational subculture is the "Generation Xers." These individuals were born between 1965 and 1980; Generation Xers number approximately 63 million in the U.S. population and are about 50 million strong in the U.S. work force.[24]

TABLE 6.3   Moral Instrumental Value Rankings by Gender

Values	Females	Males	Difference?*
Honest	1	1	
Responsible	2	2	
Loving	3	5	✓
Loyal	4	3	
Helpful	5	7	✓
Broad-minded	6	4	
Forgiving	7	6	
Polite	8	8	
Obedient	9	9	

SOURCE: Adapted from D. E. Giacomino and T. V. Eaton, "Personal values of accounting alumni: An empirical examination of differences by gender and age." *Journal of Managerial Issues* 15 (2003): 369–380.

*✓= significant gender difference on these particular values

The third subculture is the "Generation Nexters." These individuals were born between 1981 and 1999; they number approximately 60 million people in the U.S. population and 23 million in the U.S. work force.[25]

The Baby Boomers were born during or after World War II and came of age during a time of conflict and divisiveness. For example, many of them fought in the Vietnam War, and many of them fought against the Vietnam War. Many were also involved in the civil rights movement. They were associated with memorable events (e.g., Woodstock) and continue to have an influence on trends, events, and politics because of their questioning of existing policies, rules, and practices. Some general characteristics of Baby Boomers include the following:

TABLE 6.4   Competence Instrumental Value Rankings by Gender

Values	Females	Males	Difference?*
Ambitious	1	1	
Independent	2	7	✓
Capable	3	3	
Intellectual	4	4	
Courageous	5	2	✓
Logical	6	6	
Self-controlled	7	5	✓
Clean	8	9	
Imaginative	9	8	✓

SOURCE: Adapted from D. E. Giacomino and T. V. Eaton, "Personal values of accounting alumni: An empirical examination of differences by gender and age." *Journal of Managerial Issues* 15 (2003): 369–380.

*✓ = significant gender difference on these particular values

- They tend to be process oriented.
- They tend to wear their values on their sleeve.
- They tend to have an optimistic outlook.
- They tend to have a driven work ethic.
- They tend to have a love/hate view of authority.
- They tend to value relationships.
- They tend to value loyalty.
- They tend to have a team orientation.
- They tend to respect the organizational hierarchy.
- They tend to generally wait their turn for advancement.
- They tend to value stability over mobility.

The Generation Xers are the first generation of latchkey children who are products of dual-career households, or, in some 50 percent of cases, of divorced or separated parents. Because they are such a racially diverse group, they are more comfortable with diversity than any previous generation.[26] Some general characteristics of Generation Xers include the following:

- They tend to be results oriented.
- They tend to be have a skeptical outlook.
- They tend to have a balanced work ethic.
- They tend to be relatively unimpressed with authority.
- They tend to be reluctant to commit to relationships.
- They tend to be very individual in their orientation.
- They tend to be technologically literate.
- They tend to be loyal to individual managers who treat them well.
- They tend to be fiercely independent.
- They tend to want to be in control of things.
- They tend to want fast feedback.
- They tend to be into mobility, not stability.

The Generation Nexters as a group are more diverse than the Baby Boomers and the Generation Xers. According to the Center for Generational Studies, 33 percent are minorities and 25 percent have grown up in a single-parent home.[27] Some other general characteristics of Generation Nexters include the following:

- They tend to be optimistic.
- They tend to be achievement oriented.
- They tend to be open-minded.
- They tend to trust centralized authority.
- They tend to have a belief in collective action.
- They tend to be well educated.
- They tend to be very talented.
- They tend to be inclusive.
- They tend to be civic-minded.
- They tend to think globally.
- They tend to be very confident.

Generational Issues in the Workplace

Implied in the general characteristics of the three generational subcultures is that differences between them are likely to raise substantial intergenerational issues in the workplace. There are several workplace issues over which the three generational subcultures are likely to enter into conflict with one another. For example, a study of these generations at work concluded that conflicts over work ethic, loyalty, leadership, politics, and a host of other issues often arise between the different generations in the workplace.[28]

These issues suggest that the workplace has become a playing field of competing viewpoints and values as these three generational subcultures share the same workspace. Moreover, as they intersect in the workplace, their values and behaviors will inevitably come into conflict.[29] We would argue that much of this conflict can be attributed to differences in the work ethics subscribed to by the three subcultures. For example, Baby Boomers have a relentless work ethic and have been known to complain that Generation Xers lack drive and are not as committed as Baby Boomers.[30]

Studies have found that employees who possess a strong work ethic usually feel a moral commitment to achieving the types of goals that lead to organizational performance.[31] Although the three generational subcultures we discuss in this book do not share the same work ethic, it does not mean that a particular subculture's work ethic is stronger or weaker than the others' work ethic. Having said this, we must acknowledge that not all individuals in the workforce possess a strong work ethic. At the extreme, particularly for entry-level service sector jobs, Generation Xers and Generation Nexters have been described by hiring (Baby Boomer) managers as lazy, unreliable, disinterested, slow, immature, and lacking in work ethic.[32]

Offering supporting evidence for this assessment, a Texas-based human resource professional recounted his experience observing the work ethic of teenagers and college students working in a fast-food restaurant.[33] According to the observer, more than half of this group of employees were women, and one-third were minorities. The observer commented, "For me, it was an opportunity to observe the work ethic of the future work force—an ethic that amounted to a fierce aversion to hard work and a lack of respect for managers, customers, and often, coworkers." Differences in the values of these generational subcultures are implied in these observations.

Generational Values Differences

Baby Boomers have shaped much of postwar America's values, and they tend to share a number of core values that contrast significantly with the core values of Generation Xers and Generation Nexters. Below is a synopsis of each subculture's core values.

> *Core values of Baby Boomers:* prosperity, children in the spotlight, optimism, team orientation, personal gratification, consensus, health and wellness, personal growth, and youth.
> *Core values of Generation Xers:* diversity, thinking globally, balance, techno-literacy, fun, informality, self-reliance, pragmatism, and skepticism.
> *Core values of Generation Nexters:* confidence, civic duty, achievement, sociability, morality, diversity, street smarts, multiculturalism, and synergy.

Similar to studies of gender values, studies of generational values derive differences from anecdotal evidence. We again draw on the study discussed earlier in this chapter, in which gender value differences were derived from empirical analyses.[34] Recall that the authors of this study used a typology of personal values, which was developed into a value survey classifying values into two distinct categories ("instrumental" values and "terminal" values) and distinct subcategories (moral/competence instrumental values and social/personal terminal values) that represent rank-order human values.

In addition to testing for value differences between males and females, the authors also tested for value differences between younger and older individuals, where younger was defined as those participants younger than thirty-six years of age. As in the male-female study, members of the younger and older groups were asked to rank each of the values in order of impor-

TABLE 6.5   Social Terminal Value Rankings by Age Group

Values	Younger	Older	Difference?*
Family security	1	1	
True friendship	2	4	✓
Mature love	3	3	
Freedom	4	2	
Equality	5	5	
A world at peace	6	8	
Social recognition	7	7	
National security	8	6	
A world of beauty	9	9	

SOURCE: Adapted from D. E. Giacomino and T. V. Eaton, "Personal values of accounting alumni: An empirical examination of differences by gender and age." *Journal of Managerial Issues* 15 (2003): 369–380.

* ✓= significant gender difference on these particular values

tance. For each of the subcategories, they assigned a 1 to the most important value and a 9 to the least important value. The authors used the same statistical technique to determine the significance of differences between younger and older study participants on each of the values. The results are shown in Tables 6.5, 6.6, 6.7, and 6.8. The check marks in the tables indicate which of the values are significantly different between the two groups.

In the terminal values set, younger participants placed more importance on friendship (Table 6.5) and pleasure (Table 6.6). In the instrumental value set, younger participants placed more importance on being helpful (Table 6.7) and being independent (Table 6.8), and older participants

TABLE 6.6   Personal Terminal Value Rankings by Age Group

Values	Younger	Older	Difference?*
Health	1	1	
Self-respect	2	2	
Inner harmony	3	4	
Sense of accomplishment	4	5	
Salvation	5	3	
A comfortable life	6	7	
Wisdom	7	6	
Pleasure	8	9	✓
An exciting life	9	8	

SOURCE: Adapted from D. E. Giacomino and T. V. Eaton, "Personal values of accounting alumni: An empirical examination of differences by gender and age." *Journal of Managerial Issues* 15 (2003): 369–380.

* ✓ = significant gender difference on these particular values

placed more importance on being logical and imaginative (Table 6.8). These results are consistent with the core values of the three generational subcultures and empirically confirm the existence of significant differences between their values. Overall, these differences indicate that there is likely to be important value misalignments between generational subcultures within organizations.

Chapter Summary and Conclusions

At no time in history has the U.S. workforce experienced as much cross-generational diversity as exists currently. In today's organizational work-

TABLE 6.7   Moral Instrumental Value Rankings by Age Group

Values	Younger	Older	Difference?*
Honest	1	1	
Responsible	2	2	
Loving	3	5	
Loyal	4	3	
Helpful	5	7	✓
Broad-minded	6	4	
Forgiving	7	6	
Polite	8	8	
Obedient	9	9	

Source: Adapted from D. E. Giacomino and T. V. Eaton, "Personal values of accounting alumni: An empirical examination of differences by gender and age." *Journal of Managerial Issues* 15 (2003): 369–380.

* ✓ = significant gender difference on these particular values

places, cross-generational work teams will increasingly be composed of members whose histories and values are noticeably different as well as operationally different, which can lead to conflict in organizations. Inevitably, the corporate cultures of these organizations will be affected. Specifically, gender and generational value differences can lead to intergender and intergenerational behaviors that may impact an organization's ability to successfully implement the type of strategies that result in superior organizational performance.

TABLE 6.8   Competence Instrumental Value Rankings by Age Group

Values	Younger	Older	Difference?*
Ambitious	1	1	
Independent	2	6	✓
Capable	3	2	
Intellectual	4	5	
Courageous	5	3	
Logical	6	4	✓
Self-controlled	7	7	
Clean	8	9	
Imaginative	9	8	✓

SOURCE: Adapted from D. E. Giacomino and T. V. Eaton, "Personal values of accounting alumni: An empirical examination of differences by gender and age." *Journal of Managerial Issues* 15 (2003): 369–380.

* ✓= significant gender difference on these particular values

Diagnosing Corporate Culture Alignment

The preceding five chapters were conceptual in nature, in that they consisted mainly of discussions and definitions and not action items for aligning organizational subcultures. These conceptual chapters were designed to help you better understand the rationale behind the strategic change approach to aligning organizational subcultures for competitive advantage.

As discussed in Chapter 1, we view the strategic change approach to aligning organizational subcultures as a process that is vision driven, in the sense that the change is motivated by a vision that seeks to move the organization to a "better" state. We also view this approach as being values driven, in the sense that the change seeks to permeate the organization with values that build the type of team spirit that leads to a strong corporate culture—one in which organizational subcultures are aligned.

The strategic change approach begins with diagnosing an organization's corporate culture. Is it fragmented, in the sense that multiple subcultures exist? Are the subcultures aligned with the predominant corporate culture? Are the subcultures' values consistent with the predominant value system of the organization? How might these assessments be made? These are the types of questions we answer in this chapter. Before we outline the specifics of diagnosing corporate culture alignment, we discuss how to prepare employees for strategic change and all that it entails.

Prediagnostic Preparations

Because some employees in your organizations may have been involved with change efforts in the past, perhaps with little or no success, they may be skeptical about impending change efforts. Therefore, it is very important that a proper foundation for change is constructed prior to implementing change. Such a foundation prepares employees to cope with both the positive and negative effects of the impending change by fostering a healthy and productive climate for change. With respect to providing information to employees about the impending strategic change, members of your organization's top management team can construct this foundation by doing the following:

1. Develop a plan that provides particulars about the strategic change. (At a minimum, the plan should specify reasons for the change, the diagnostic process, and the expected outcomes.)
2. Ensure that those who will or might be directly (employees) and indirectly (for example, client organizations) affected by the change are informed about what is going on and how it may affect them.
3. Provide those who will or might be affected with information that will reduce their uncertainty and ambiguity regarding the change.
4. Communicate this information as early as possible to pre-empt damaging rumors and to ensure that incorrect, anxiety-provoking information does not spread.
5. Provide forums for employees to communicate their reactions and concerns about the impending change to the top management team.

As a way of building on the constructed foundation, members of the organization's top management team should communicate, both verbally and through their actions, the following to employees:

1. They understand the emotional implications of the impending strategic change.
2. They are personally committed to the change.
3. They recognize that the change might have negative impacts upon some employees.
4. They are open to discussion of the feelings of employees regarding the impending change.
5. They are confident that the "team" can make it through the change.
6. They want and need input from employees to make the change work.

As a general recommendation, the top management team should communicate as much information as possible about the change to employees. Communication should be designed to decrease resistance and encourage moving through the change effectively and positively.

Diagnostic Approaches

Since diagnosing subculture alignment is the first step in the strategic change approach, ample time should be spent preparing employees for the approach that will be used to conduct the diagnosis. In this section, we present the strategic change agents with three approaches to diagnosing whether, or the degree to which, organizational subcultures are in alignment. These include the survey approach, the interview approach, and the observation approach. Once the approach to be used is selected, employees should be informed about the process.

The Survey Approach

Diagnosing corporate culture requires collecting data, and the survey approach is probably the most frequently used data-gathering device. Although surveys designed to diagnose corporate culture can be administered to employees by the traditional method of paper and pencil, the electronic survey may be the preferred method. Whether you choose to use the traditional method or the electronic method, there are four steps involved in using the survey approach: (1) designing the survey, (2) administering the survey, (3) analyzing the survey results, and (4) providing feedback.

Designing the Survey. A well-designed survey will produce the type of data that will be useful in diagnosing whether organizational subcultures are in alignment. Capturing relevant demographic information is a hallmark of a well-designed survey. In the case of organizational subcultures, the survey should have an opening section that asks employees to provide demographic data such as gender, age, racial/cultural background, job title, and other information that will facilitate diagnosing corporate culture. A typical format for collecting this type of data might resemble the survey shown in Box 7.1.

In terms of gathering the type of data that will provide insights into whether organizational subcultures are in alignment, there are several dimensions of culture that can be assessed in a survey. In Chapter 2 we listed seven dimensions of corporate culture.[1]

1. *Individual autonomy.* The degree of responsibility, independence, and opportunity for exercising initiative that individuals in the organization have
2. *Structure.* The number of rules and regulations and the amount of direct supervision that is used to oversee and control employee behavior
3. *Support.* The degree of assistance and warmth provided by managers to their subordinates
4. *Identification.* The degree to which members identify with the organization as a whole rather than with their particular work group or field of professional expertise
5. *Performance reward.* The degree to which reward allocations (for example, salary increase or promotion) are based on employee performance criteria
6. *Conflict tolerance.* The degree of conflict present in relationships between peers and work groups as well as the willingness to be honest and open about differences

BOX 7.1

SECTION 1: Demographic Information

A. Gender (please check the appropriate box):

☐ Male ☐ Female
(This information will help you identify gender subcultures.)

B. Age _____
(This information will help you identify generational subcultures.)

C. Ethnic Classification (please check the appropriate box):

☐ American Indian/Alaska Native ☐ Asian
☐ Black/African American ☐ Pacific Islander
☐ Hispanic/Latino ☐ White
(This information will help you identify racial and ethnic subcultures.)

D. Department Name: _____
(This information will help you identify occupational subcultures.)

E. Job Title: _____
(This information will help you further define occupational subcultures.)

F. How long have you been employed by this corporation?_____

G. How long have you been in the department/unit in which you are currently working? _____
(Information from items E and F will help you decide whether to include in your analysis those employees who have only been with the organization/department a short time.)

---

7. *Risk tolerance.* The degree to which employees are encouraged to be aggressive, innovative, and risk seeking

These dimensions can be incorporated into a survey that can provide information about the alignment or misalignment of organizational subcultures. That is, they will indicate the extent to which individuals in each subculture agree or disagree that the organization adheres to these dimensions. In administering such a survey, employees are first provided with a description of the seven dimensions and then asked to respond to statements about each of the dimensions relative to their experience in the organization. Employees respond to items on the survey using a scale that ranges from strongly agree to strongly disagree, using a five-point scale, where "Strongly Agree" = 5 points, "Agree" = 4 points, "Neutral" = 3 points, "Disagree" = 2 points, and "Strongly Disagree" = 1 point. An example is shown in Box 7.2.

The survey shown in Box 7.2 provides information on general dimensions of corporate culture. Another type of survey can be designed to provide information about vision and values. Since the strategic change approach is driven by vision and values, this type of survey gets to the heart of the matter by assessing the extent to which organizational vision and values are understood and shared by subcultures within the organization. Items in this survey (Box 7.3) were adapted from a survey that was developed by Dr. G. James Francis, Colorado State University.

These two examples of surveys suggest what types of questions might be asked to measure the extent to which organizational subcultures are in alignment. Of course, you can develop your own survey items that are tailored to your organization's unique situation. Alternatively, you may want to consult with organizations that are in the business of helping other organizations to develop surveys to diagnose corporate culture alignment.[2]

Administering the Survey.　Some basic practicalities need to be considered before administering the survey. Foremost among these practicalities is informing employees about the purpose of the survey, what information you seek to obtain from the survey data, and how the information will be used. Things to be considered include how this information will be

BOX 7.2

Please express your feeling about the statements provided below by circling one of the following responses:

- Strongly Agree (SA)
- Agree (A)
- Neutral (N)
- Disagree (D)
- Strongly Disagree (SD)

1. Employees are given a high degree of individual autonomy to perform their job in this organization:

    SA A N D SD

2. Employees are subject to a high degree of structure while performing their job in this organization:

    SA A N D SD

3. Employees are provided with a high degree of support while performing their job in this organization:

    SA A N D SD

4. Employees exhibit a high degree of identification with this organization:

    SA A N D SD

5. Employees perceive there to be a high degree of association between performance and rewards in this organization:

    SA A N D SD

6. Employees perceive there to be a high degree of conflict tolerance between them and their coworkers in this organization:

    SA A N D SD

7. Employees perceive there to be a high degree of risk tolerance in this organization:

    SA A N D SD

BOX 7.3

Please circle the number that best represents your response to each question:

1. To what extent do you understand and share the organization's vision?
   Not at all   **Completely**
   1   **2**   **3**   **4**   **5**   **6**   **7**   **8**   **9**   **10**

2. To what extent do you understand and share the organization's values?
   Not at all   **Completely**
   1   **2**   **3**   **4**   **5**   **6**   **7**   **8**   **9**   **10**

3. To what extent do you share the organization's values for customer service?
   Not at all   **Completely**
   1   **2**   **3**   **4**   **5**   **6**   **7**   **8**   **9**   **10**

4. To what extent do you share the organization's values for technological development and implementation?
   Not at all   **Completely**
   1   **2**   **3**   **4**   **5**   **6**   **7**   **8**   **9**   **10**

5. To what extent do you share the organization's values regarding the treatment of employees?
   Not at all   **Completely**
   1   **2**   **3**   **4**   **5**   **6**   **7**   **8**   **9**   **10**

6. To what extent do you share the organization's values for risk taking?
   Not at all   **Completely**
   1   **2**   **3**   **4**   **5**   **6**   **7**   **8**   **9**   **10**

7. To what extent is organizational learning an important value for you?
   Not at all   **Completely**
   1   **2**   **3**   **4**   **5**   **6**   **7**   **8**   **9**   **10**

8. To what extent do you share the organization's values for creativity and innovation?
   Not at all   **Completely**
   1   **2**   **3**   **4**   **5**   **6**   **7**   **8**   **9**   **10**

9. To what extent do you share the organization's communication values?
   Not at all   **Completely**
   1   **2**   **3**   **4**   **5**   **6**   **7**   **8**   **9**   **10**

10. To what extent do you share the organization's values for trust?
    Not at all   **Completely**
    1   **2**   **3**   **4**   **5**   **6**   **7**   **8**   **9**   **10**

11. To what extent do you share the organization's values for change?
    Not at all   **Completely**
    1   **2**   **3**   **4**   **5**   **6**   **7**   **8**   **9**   **10**

---

disseminated to employees and who will disseminate the information. Will employees be informed by e-mail, department meeting, newsletter, or some other medium? Will the CEO inform employees, their department manager, or some other person(s) in the organization?

Once these types of questions are answered, other issues will need to be resolved. Typical questions include the following:

1. *Will the survey be administered to a sample of employees or to the population of employees?* The answer to this question might depend on the size of your organization and the financial and technological resources available. For example, a small organization might be able to survey all of its employees, whereas a large organization might want to administer the survey to a selected sample of employees from each subculture. However, if your organization has intranet capabilities and can administer the survey using this technology, our recommendation is that the entire population of employees be surveyed.

2. *Will the survey be mailed to employees' homes?* If this option is selected, be prepared to deal with additional cost issues such as providing self-addressed, stamped envelopes for returning the survey and follow-up mailings for nonrespondents.

3. *Will the survey be administered to employees during working hours?* If this option is selected, the main issue is determining the most convenient time to administer the survey. Another issue to be resolved is deciding whether employees will respond to the survey privately or in a group setting at some specified located within the organization. This issue may be easily resolved in organizations that have intranet capabilities. In any case, you will need to make practical arrangements for administering the survey.

4. *How long will it take to administer the survey?* This question can be answered by pre-testing the survey, perhaps using a group of managers. Pre-testing will help you determine the time it takes to administer, process, and analyze the survey and will also help you clear out some of the bugs that may be in the survey.

5. *Who will administer the survey?* The answer to this question identifies not only the specific individuals who will administer the

survey but also the procedures to be followed in formatting, reproducing, distributing, and collecting the surveys once they have been completed by employees.

6. *What procedures will be used for assuring the confidentiality of the information collected from the survey?* These procedures can be explained to employees by their immediate supervisor or through some organization-wide communication system (newsletter, e-mail). On the survey itself, it is important that employees are informed that their responses will remain anonymous. This increases the chances that employees will respond candidly to the survey.

Analyzing the Results. Once the surveys have been completed and re-turned, the data must be first prepared and then analyzed. Data preparation includes recording the receipt of mail surveys (or electronic surveys), coding the data, editing the data, tabulating the data, and preparing survey reports.

Data analysis can include simple statistical procedures such as calculation of averages and frequency distributions for specific survey questions. In addition, differences in survey results among organizational subcultures may be examined using standard statistical tests. For example, the F-test may be used to determine whether the average survey response of any subcultures differ significantly from that of other subcultures.

The F-test tests the hypothesis that all subculture means (averages) are equal. The F-test will be significant if at least one subculture's mean response on the survey items is statistically different from any other subculture's mean response. If the F-test indicates that there are significant differences, this result would suggest that the subcultures are not aligned. A series of t-tests may be conducted to identify which subcultures are different from other subcultures. The t-test tests the hypothesis that two specific subculture means are significantly different from each other. A significant t-test indicates that the two subcultures represent two populations with different means.[3]

Regardless of the statistical analyses performed, the display of survey findings is important. Statistical graphs should accompany narrative text to aid comparison and interpretation. For example, bar graphs and comparison charts visually demonstrate meaningful differences among subcultures.

Providing Feedback. This is the final component of the survey approach. Although there is no established format for providing feedback to employees about a survey's results, there are several things that should be considered prior to proceeding with this task. One consideration concerns the type of feedback that will be provided. At a minimum, feedback might include providing employees with contextual information, for example, a review of why the survey was conducted, a presentation of how the survey was conducted, an explanation of the survey instrument itself, a presentation of the quantified results, a discussion of the results, and how the results will be used.

Another consideration is whether to provide the feedback to all employees at one large meeting or hold several meetings with small groups of employees. The former option ensures that all employees will hear the same information at the same time. Although the latter approach has its advantages (for example, it will facilitate greater employee interaction about the change and may help them develop a sense of team), it may not promote feedback consistency, and there may be some employees in the group who will not feel comfortable sharing their feelings about the impending change in a small group context. The more "personal" the effects of the change, the more likely these employees will withdraw from the group process.

Yet another consideration is determining who will provide the feedback. Because the subject of change can be sensitive, the feedback process needs to be managed with skill and expertise. While expression of concerns about change are healthy, one or two particularly vocal and negative employees can set the tone for the group and can cause the feedback process to become destructive. If the internal change agent (for example, manager) does not feel that he or she possesses the requisite skills or expertise, utilizing an external facilitator may be necessary.

A final consideration is deciding whether the feedback will be presented to employees in a written or an oral format. Given the potential for change to create emotions in the workplace, it is wise to use both a written and an oral format to provide feedback to employees. However, the more it is perceived that the change may create emotional reactions, the more important it is to use the oral format first. A written format to provide feedback can be used as a backup.

The Interview Approach

The interview approach can be carried out through individual interviews or focus group interviews. Whether the interviews are conducted in a group or individual format, several interviewers may be required (especially if your organization is large). These interviewers should be trained as a group to ensure standardization and control. This training, for the most part, should focus on ensuring that each interviewer is well acquainted with the interview questions and that they all have ample practice asking the questions in mock interviews.

As for the type of questions the interviewers should ask, the same questions used in the survey approach can be asked during the interview. In fact, it may be wise to use these closed-ended survey questions rather than asking open-ended questions. When using the latter, you will need to make a decision about how much of the employees' responses should be recorded, how much the interviewer should "probe" for responses, and how much the interviewer should account for context (for example, employee age, race, gender, reaction to the study, and so on).

The Observation Approach

Throughout this book we have conveyed the message that a strong corporate culture is one where organizational subcultures are aligned, and a weak corporate culture is one where organizational subcultures are misaligned. Moreover, a strong corporate culture is one where the organization conducts its business according to a clear set of values, management devotes considerable time to communicating these values to employees, and these values are shared widely across the organization by senior executives and rank-and-file employees alike.[4] In contrast, a weak corporate culture is one where few values are widely shared, there is little cohesion across organizational departments, and employees have no deeply felt sense of corporate identity.[5]

Essentially, when attempting to determine whether organizational sub-cultures are aligned (strong corporate culture) or misaligned (weak corporate culture), the change agent can make a diagnosis through observation of particular symptoms. The observation approach has several benefits. First, the diagnosis is likely to be more accurate than the interview, survey, or any other approach (we will say more about this later). Second, the observation approach takes up less of employees' time. Third, we feel that this approach is less disruptive, in terms of evoking employee concerns about why a diagnosis is needed and how it might impact them or their job. However, there are some drawbacks in using this approach: (1) the skill level of the individual doing the observing must be high to obtain an accurate diagnosis; and (2) if the organization is large, over one hundred employees, it may require several observers to get the job done in a timely fashion.

As a general rule, when using the observation approach to diagnosing corporate culture, you should observe what is said and done within the organization. The key to this approach is to disregard your biases and beliefs, to try not to evaluate, and to record only what you see and hear. Symptoms of weak corporate culture may be quite clear or very subtle. Subtle symptoms of weak corporate culture include the following:[6]

- Employees do not respond to the organization's external environment but simply work to get ahead or to keep superiors happy.
- Employees tend to have a short-term focus; long-term organizational interests are sacrificed to meet short-term targets.
- Employees avoid showing or sharing their feelings or emotions.
- Employees depersonalize issues (for example, they never point the finger at anyone in particular).
- Employees never challenge those in authority and always wait for them to take the initiative in resolving their problems.
- Employees are very conservative in their actions and take a "better the devil you know" attitude.
- Employees tend to have an isolationist attitude, where the sentiment is "do your own thing and avoid stepping on other people's toes."

- Employees tend to possess strong feelings of aversion or repugnance toward one another.

At the other end of the continuum, clear symptoms of weak corporate culture include the following:[7]

- *Morale problems.* Increasing or high turnover may indicate that something is wrong with the way the organization treats its employees.
- *Fragmentation and inconsistency.* Rather than having a unified corporate culture, the organization has several subcultures, which may be visible in different standards of dress or work habits among employees.
- *Emotional outbursts.* Weak corporate cultures leave employees uncertain, insecure, and anxious. They are manifested by emotional outbursts in the workplace or by personal problems of employees.

Other activities that can round out the observation approach include the following:[8]

- *Observe the physical setting of the organization.* Organizations with strong corporate culture provide uniformly good (not necessarily plush) facilities for all employees, and organizations with weak corporate cultures tend to differentiate facilities, with some employees having poor facilities relative to what is provided for other employees.
- *Read what the organization writes.* Organizations with strong corporate culture tend to make statements about their values without being apologetic, and organizations with weak corporate cultures use such communications to discuss business performance in conventional financial form (balance sheets, income statements, and so on).

Pros and Cons of the Three Diagnostic Approaches

The Traditional Survey Approach (Pros)

- Surveys are a relatively inexpensive mode of data collection.
- Surveys can be administered by a relatively unskilled individual.
- Surveys can be mailed to employees.
- Surveys present a uniform stimulus to all employees (that is, each employee receives an identical survey).
- The anonymity that often accompanies the survey may result in employees being more open and truthful in their responses.[9]

The Traditional Survey Approach (Cons)

- Employees may not complete the entire survey; the missing data will complicate statistical analyses.
- Response rate may be a problem if the survey is mailed to employees; some employees may not respond if the survey is administered on-line.
- The survey approach can be inflexible in that employees are unable to explain fully their attitudes, values, opinions, and so on.[10]

The Electronic Survey Approach (Pros)

- It is less expensive to administer the survey on-line than to pay for postage or incur the costs associated with using internal interviewers.
- It is easier to make changes to the survey items and to copy and sort data.
- The surveys can be delivered to employees in seconds, rather than in days as with traditional mail.
- You may send invitations and receive responses in a very short time and thus receive estimates of the level of employee participation.

- Response rates on private networks are higher with electronic surveys than with paper surveys or interviews.
- Employees may answer more honestly with electronic surveys than with paper surveys or interviews.
- Due to the speed of on-line networks, employees can answer in minutes or hours, and coverage can be global.[11]

The Electronic Survey Approach (Cons)

- The response rate will be limited to those employees with access to a computer and the organization's on-line network.
- Due to the open nature of most on-line networks, it is difficult to guarantee anonymity and confidentiality.
- More instruction and orientation to the computer on-line systems may be necessary for respondents to complete the questionnaire.
- Computers have a much greater likelihood of "glitches" than oral or written forms of communication.
- E-mail response rates may be higher than traditional response rates only during the first few days; thereafter, the rates may not be significantly higher.[12]

The Interview Approach (Pros)

- A higher percentage of employees are likely to agree to be interviewed than the percentage who will return a completed survey.
- Interviews can be more flexible than surveys if the questions are open-ended. Even if they are closed-ended, employees may be afforded the opportunity to express their opinions.
- The validity of an employee's response to an interview question may be assessed to a greater extent than when the survey approach is used.[13]

The Interview Approach (Cons)

- The interview approach is generally more costly than the survey approach and the observation approach.
- Although the interview approach may be useful for "probing" into employees' attitudes, the interpersonal nature of this approach may actually lead to changes in employee attitudes.
- The training of interviewers can be a long and costly process.
- Because of fatigue or decreased interest, the interviewer is prone to altering the manner in which questions are posed to employees.
- The characteristics (for example, gender, race, culture, and so on) of the interviewer and of those being interviewed may influence responses to the questions being asked.[14]

The Observation Approach (Pros)

- The observer can often obtain data about behavior that employees may be either unwilling or unable to report themselves.
- Employee behavior is observed as it occurs.[15]

The Observation Approach (Cons)

- Observers may provide incomplete reports of what they observe.
- Observers often require considerable training, which can be expensive and time-consuming.
- The observer must be present when the behavior is actually exhibited, which can be costly in terms of time and money.[16]

Chapter Summary and Conclusions

Diagnosing corporate culture to determine whether organizational sub-cultures are aligned or misaligned is a very important step in the strategic change approach. In this chapter, we have outlined three diagnostic approaches—the survey approach, the interview approach, and the observation approach. Under the survey approach, we discussed how surveys are designed, provided representative samples of surveys that can be used for diagnosing corporate culture, suggested methods for analyzing the surveys, and set forth some considerations for providing employees with survey feedback. Under the interview approach, our focus was on ensuring standardization and control, and under the observation approach, we emphasized that the observer must disregard his or her biases and beliefs in order to collect data that is used for aligning subcultures. Finally, we analyzed the advantages and disadvantages of each approach.

Assessing Strategic Vision

If one were to do a cursory examination of management literature and talk to a broad cross-section of business executives, it would soon become clear that vision is a term that is commonly used but often misunderstood. Although most contributors to the discussion realize that vision is important, it is often poorly defined and misapplied. For example, in one study consisting of one national and three regional samples of 331 chief executive respondents, only one CEO was able to put his vision statement in writing when all were asked to do so by comparing their organization's own vision against scholarly definitions of vision.[1] Even worse, in many organizations, most employees are unaware of their organization's vision altogether. In these companies it is unreasonable to expect people to accept, believe, and passionately work to make the vision a reality. In the context of aligning organizational subcultures, vision serves a fundamentally important and central role.

That the importance of vision can be a powerful and motivating force is not controversial. Vision can play a major role in the evolution of societies, companies, and individual lives. In his book, *The Fifth Discipline*, Peter Senge recounts a scene from the end of the movie *Spartacus* that depicts the struggles of a Roman slave turned gladiator (played by Kirk Douglas) who led an outmanned army of slaves against the Roman Empire in 71 B.C.[2] Despite early successes, they were eventually conquered by the Roman army, led by General Marcus Crassus. In the scene, Crassus tells the defeated remnants of Spartacus' army (still numbering in the thousands): "You have been slaves. You will be slaves again. But you will be spared your rightful punishment of crucifixion by the mercy of Roman legions. All you need to do is turn over to me the slave Spartacus, because we do not know him by sight."

After a period of silence, Spartacus steps forward and identifies himself. Then another man stands up and claims that he is Spartacus. Then another man and another and another does the same. In a short time, the entire defeated band follows suit, and in the process, each seals his own fate. In effect, they choose death over lives as slaves. The vision that Spartacus created and that his renegade army briefly experienced—that they could be free men—is sufficiently compelling that no one is willing to abandon it and return to a life of slavery.

A more contemporary example of vision comes from the civil rights movement, which became an unstoppable force for societal change in the United States in the 1960s. One of the defining moments of the civil rights movement occurred on August 28, 1963, when, on the steps of the Lincoln Memorial in Washington, D.C., Martin Luther King Jr. delivered his famous "I Have a Dream" speech. In the speech, King outlined a vision for America that engaged and mobilized a nation that had grown increasingly dissatisfied with the status quo. After identifying some of the shortcomings that continued to persist, King outlined his vision for the country:

> I have a dream that one day this nation will rise up and live out the true meaning of its creed: "We hold these truths to be self-evident: that all men are created equal." I have a dream that one day on the red hills of Georgia the sons of former slaves and the sons of former slave owners will be able to sit down together at a table of brotherhood. I have a dream that one day even the state of Mississippi, a desert state, sweltering with the heat of injustice and oppression, will be transformed into an oasis of freedom and justice. I have a dream that my four children will one day live in a nation where they will not be judged by the color of their skin but by the content of their character. I have a dream today.

I have a dream that one day the state of Alabama, whose governor's lips are presently dripping with the words of interposition and nullification, will be transformed into a situation where little black boys and little black girls will be able to join hands with little white boys and little white girls and walk together as sisters and brothers. I have a dream today. I have a dream that one day every valley shall be exalted, every hill and mountain shall be made low, the rough places will be made plain, and the crooked places will be made straight, and the glory of the Lord shall be revealed, and the flesh shall see it together. This is our hope. This is the faith with which I return to the South. With this faith, we will be able to hew out of the mountain of despair a stone of hope. With this faith we will be able to transform the jangling discord of our nation into a beautiful symphony of brotherhood. With this faith we will be able to work together, to pray together, to struggle together, to go to jail together, to stand up for freedom together, knowing that one day we will be free . . .

The powerful images that these words created galvanized many Americans and moved them to commit themselves to the cause. It was clear that before the civil rights movement, America had not lived up to its promise and that much work remained to be done. It also became clear that the difficulties that lay ahead were deemed by many to be worth the cost. The vision of a better and more just country passionately inspired citizens to take up the cause and make it happen.

A clear and convincing vision can also lay the foundation of success in the business world. When Jack Welch assumed the top spot at General Electric in 1981, GE was a successful company, but Welch was convinced that it was not realizing its full potential. To unlock that potential, Welch began a radical revolution that left no one at GE untouched. By the time Welch had finished, many of GE's businesses had been eliminated, almost one-third of its workers had lost their jobs, and the way GE did business had changed. This was not done in a random or haphazard way, however. Welch had a vision for the company that rested on the notion of competitiveness. In fact, he pursued a vision in which GE's businesses needed to be the number-one or number-two company *in the world* in the industries they competed in (and most of the businesses were number one!).[3]

In a *Harvard Business Review* interview about a decade after he was named CEO, Welch was asked the question, "What makes a good manager?" He responded, "I prefer the term business leader. Good business leaders create a vision, articulate the vision, passionately own the vision, and relentlessly drive it to completion."[4] This is what he had done at GE, but it is worth noting that before significant change occurred, the organization, in Welch's mind, had been redefined by a new and radically different vision. Once the vision was in place, Welch began to promote a set of values that eventually permeated the organization. Commitment to these values was not obtained quickly, but over time the relentless pursuit of them helped an entrenched bureaucratic organization recreate itself.

As the above examples demonstrate, vision can be a powerful and motivating force for unifying people and inducing change. Although a strong and positive vision is one of those "We know it when we see it" concepts, there are some things that companies can do to ensure that their visioning process results in the desired outcomes.

What Vision Is Not

As stated above, vision is often misunderstood and misapplied. Too often, companies roll out a vision statement that is a confusing mix of values, philosophies, goals, strategies, priorities, initiatives, and business practices. While they often sound good, they generally have little impact on the organization or the decisions that are made. Thus, before we begin to discuss what vision is, why it is important, and how an effective vision can be developed, we think it is useful to discuss what vision is not. This discussion will focus on how the concept has been misused in the past and why, sadly, many decision makers think that vision is not important.

Perhaps the most widely cited example of a corporate chieftain to disavow vision was Louis V. Gerstner Jr. of IBM, who confidently proclaimed to the world shortly after taking the company's reigns in 1993, "The last thing IBM needs right now is a vision."[5] Instead, he argued that IBM needed textbook "blocking and tackling"—lower costs and better market focus across its divisions. Although one could argue that the latter sentiment contains at least the underpinnings of a vision, Gerstner was roundly criticized for lack of leadership at a time when the company needed it most. Gerstner was equating vision with being a visionary. He believed that a visionary maneuvered in the realm of the obscure, the abstract, the impractical, and the unimportant. Vision, to him, was an academic exercise that really didn't translate to the company or its bottom line. The focus on the bottom line was somewhat revealing in that it reflected Gerstner's background as an accountant. When he became CEO, he was both a corporate and industry outsider. The one thing he knew how to do, and the one thing that is generally transparent across industries, is cost reduction. It requires very little industry understanding and very little creativity.

This view was not widely shared by others at the time; in fact, others within Gerstner's core industry believed that vision was important to their own companies. For example, UNISYS's chairman at the time, James Unruh, believed that for his company to survive and prosper (it had been on the brink of bankruptcy), a major reorganization of the company needed to be undertaken—one that included a fundamental shift in the idea of how value was created. Similarly, at Wang Laboratories, a major shift in focus was initiated based on the CEO's vision of what the company needed to become to compete successfully in the future. Scott McNealy of Sun Microsystems, IBM's competitor in workstations, argued that vision was crucial, especially at larger companies, because it provided a focus that people throughout the organization could use to help make compatible decisions.[6]

Vision is not a financial target—like stringing together enough satisfactory quarters for CEOs to hold onto their jobs—or any other short-term target or goal. Performance should logically follow the successful implementation of a viable long-term vision, but it is not the vision in and of itself. Vision is bigger and broader and is achieved over a longer period of time than traditional business goals.

Visions are also not a one-time, lone-wolf effort. Executives who believe that once they create a vision their duties end, and the responsibility to implement their dictum is discharged to their subordinates, are in for a rude awakening. This approach is usually superficial and is unlikely to engender any kind of common mind-set or inspire people throughout the organization to achieve it. And when a single person (or even small group) develops the vision, it is often hard to get others to embrace it. This isn't to say that visions don't or can't come about as the result of a top-down process, but rather that sometimes visions can and should come from other places in the organization. If a vision is good and could result in a better and more competitive organization, the origin of the idea should be a secondary consideration. Senge makes the point that it is presumptuous to assume that a leader's vision should be the organization's vision and that this automatically will be accepted. At the end of the day, a leader's vision is a personal vision, and it does not become a positive and powerful source for change unless and until it becomes widely shared by people throughout the organization.[7] To the extent that employees have been involved in the process, the likelihood that they will commit themselves to making it happen is greater.

Neither is vision a solution to a problem. In many organizations, initiatives are undertaken to solve a problem, and when the problem goes away, so do the energy and interest that were needed to take it on. Vision is much more focused on the future. A vision is really never attained because, for forward-looking leaders, the closer they get to a vision, the further it is pushed away as new information forces a continual re-evaluation of what the organization is trying to become.

Finally, a vision is not an advertising slogan or catchy phrase. To reduce a vision to either of these is to completely miss the point. While it is important that people understand and internalize the vision, there are ways to accomplish this other than making the vision short and catchy. The defining characteristic of a company's vision should not be that it looks good on a t-shirt, but rather that it embodies some of the organization's enduring fundamental beliefs.

James Lucas has identified a number of flaws that render a vision statement worthless. Although stated in an ironic tone, the underlying issues are real:

• Make it so generic that it has little meaning. "Simply world class" was a vision that was actually adopted by one company. The company conducted focus groups to find out what the vision meant to individual employees and they got almost as many answers as they had employees.

- Go for lofty wording that doesn't touch anyone, but instead makes them wonder if management is "touched." "We are an amazing organization made up of outstanding employees who provide our terrific customers with unbelievable products and services. God bless us, every one."
- Focus on statistics (for example, increased productivity, profitability, or market share) rather than the core values and competencies that lead to those results. "We will deliver long-term earnings growth and shareholder value." Hardly the kind of stuff that stirs the passions of employees and makes them willing to sacrifice for the good of the cause.
- Write what you think ought to be done rather than what you truly want to do or can reasonably accomplish. In other words, check creativity and passion at the door.
- Leave people out of the process. When you want their opinion, you'll give it to them.
- Think of vision as an "initiative" rather than as a resolution of your identity. This type of thinking relegates vision to a project to be accomplished rather than a journey to understanding the organization and what its potential might be.
- Ignore your core values. Core values are important to any organization and a company's vision should reflect them. Let's hope the organization has some.
- Make it too long and detailed, or too short and terse. If a vision statement is too long and/or contains too much detail, it drifts toward the status of a plan or a list of priorities. In these cases it loses its "timeless" nature and looks more like a short-term agenda. For example, one Arizona metropolitan area had written a seventeen-page vision. How would you like to tackle that! If a vision statement is too short or terse, it ceases to provide any guidance to employees and runs the risk of being relegated to "slogan" status. In these cases the complexities and uniqueness of the organization are generally ignored.[8]

If a vision suffers from the above flaws, it will probably be viewed as more fiction than fact. A flawed vision can have a detrimental impact on an organization, as it can lead to lower employee morale and long-term ineffectiveness. This is especially likely to occur when actual practice and the vision are contradictory. Some signs that a company's corporate vision is fiction, or an illusion, include the following:

- It's never brought up in strategy or planning sessions.
- Employees who have been with the company for more than thirty days can't express what the vision means to them or how it relates to their daily priorities or decisions.
- The company finishes the "vision thing" and moves on to other projects or initiatives, forgetting that the vision is neither a project nor an initiative.
- The absence of ongoing dialogue, employee training, and development of the vision are all clues that it is just an illusion.
- When given the chance for anonymous input on the company's vision, employees suggest that the vision sounds good but is useless or meaningless.[9]

What Vision Is and Why It Is Important

Vision, as the name implies, refers to the ability to see. For businesses, it is the organization's ability to see what it will look like at some point in the future. A fairly clinical definition of vision is that it is a description, or mental image, of what the organization should be in the future, based on commonly shared values and perceptions of the organization and its environment, which is persuasively communicated to organizational members by its leaders.

Beyond this definition, several points should be noted about an organization's vision. First, vision is a future-focused concept. It is based on an idea of what the organization should look like in the future. As there are very few facts about the future, visions must be perceived because they cannot be observed. Vision is more than simply a larger reflection of what an organization is at present. Unlike strategies, visions are not grounded in a detailed analysis of an organization's current competencies or environmental conditions but rather encompass a long-term view of what the organization would like to be, given the environment that one might expect to exist at some future point in time. Visions transcend current conditions and are, instead, based on positive and growth-oriented themes that force an organization to redefine itself.

Second, visions are shaped, to a large degree, by a firm's core values. Those companies with a weak (or nonexistent) core find it especially difficult to define what they should become because they don't have a very clear understanding of what they are. Core values, which are discussed in more detail in Chapter 9, are those basic principles and philosophies that are enduring in nature. They do not change like a company's strategic intent. Values that are deeply held and widely shared by people throughout the organization provide a foundation upon which to construct a mental image of what the organization will look like in the future. Values provide the passion and persuasion that is necessary to facilitate the kind of change that a vision usually requires.

Third, to the extent that an organizational vision is shared, it becomes a powerful and motivating force for positive change and progress. Senge notes that a shared vision is more than an idea; it is a force in people's hearts. And even though it may be inspired by an idea, once it becomes shared, it is more than an abstraction because people begin to see it as though it exists.[10] The challenge for organizations is to clearly and passionately articulate the vision and persuade employees to embrace it. When an organization has many competing ideas about what it should do and what it should become, there is internal chaos and confusion. Although all leaders in the organization need a conception of what their own department needs to do to succeed, it must be compatible with the organization's overall vision.

A final point about vision is that it is inextricably tied to leadership. In fact, it is difficult to discuss either vision or leadership without mentioning the other. A common belief among employees is that corporations are overmanaged and underled. One of the defining characteristics of effective leaders is their ability to create a viable vision for their organizations and then create a structure that is capable of achieving that vision. Leaders create visions that go beyond themselves. They care deeply about their organizations, and they are out in front, charting a course and then pulling the organization along with them rather than pushing the organization from behind.

A framework that we find useful for discussing vision is one developed by Collins and Poras.[11] They argue that a well-conceived vision has two parts: core ideology and envisioned future. Core ideology is the conceptual glue that holds an organization together as it grows and deals with the ongoing issues that it must confront. Core ideology deals with a company's core values and core purpose. Although the distinction between core values and core purpose may seem trivial, it is not. Core purpose is a powerful statement about why the organization exists. It is not a business goal. Rather, it embraces a notion that is larger than the organization or anyone in it. A company that has a true sense of how it fits into the overall scheme of things lets people know why the work they do is important.

Core purpose defines how an organization improves people's lives and contributes to society or the human condition. It is a grand concept that makes people want to get out of bed in the morning and put in a good day's work. It is never achieved but it is always there as something to strive for. For example, the core purpose of Cargill is to improve the standard of living around the world; the core purpose of Mary Kay Cosmetics is to give unlimited opportunity to women; Merck's is to preserve and improve human life; Sony's is to experience the joy of advancing and applying technology for the benefit of the public; Walt Disney's is to make people happy. Core values, on the other hand, have great intrinsic value and, as mentioned above, are fundamentally important to people throughout the organization because they define what ideals are fundamental to the organization and non-negotiable in the conduct of business.

Core ideology is not a differentiator between one company and another. It is quite possible that two or more organizations could have the same core purpose or core values. Furthermore, core ideology is important only to people within the organization because it lays the foundation for creating and maintaining the passion necessary to do great things.

The second part of Collins and Poras's vision framework is envisioned future, and it consists of two elements: a "big hairy audacious goal" and a vivid description of the future desired state of the organization. When creating a vision-level goal (which may take from ten to thirty years to accomplish), companies must think beyond current capabilities and the current environment. A long-term goal involves an understanding of what the organization can excel at, what drives its economic engine, and what people in the organization will be passionate about. It is not reck-lessly based in ego, but rather a thorough understanding of these three things.[12] Having this type of long-term goal engages people and helps to focus their effort and attention. It also helps them to make decisions be-cause when the end is unambiguous and compelling, the decisions that must be made along the way to making it a reality become clear.

A vivid description reinforces the vision by describing in detail what it will be like when the organization achieves it. This element is analogous to an artist painting a picture. The more detail the artist provides, the less interpretation a viewer of the work needs to have in order to understand and appreciate it. A vivid description paints the picture of what it will be like to achieve the long-term goal. As illustrated in the examples at the be-ginning of this chapter, a vivid description of the vision often requires the use of passion, emotion, and conviction on the part of the leader.

There are many reasons that an organization should invest in the devel-opment of an effective long-term vision. First, a well-crafted vision clari-fies the direction for change. Vision to a company is similar to the North Star to sailors. For centuries this reference point safely guided sailors to their destinations. Vision is a clear and constant reference point that is fixed in an organization's psyche. It is about possibilities, not probabili-ties. Probabilities tell us what is likely to happen. Possibilities are about identifying what can happen if the organization has the foresight and for-titude to make change happen. And when a vision becomes internalized, it continually reminds people about what they are trying to accomplish together and what the organization is striving to become.

Second, a well-developed vision will motivate and inspire people throughout the organization to passionately contribute to its achievement. To the extent that more and more people buy into the large concept, there is less and less room for those that don't accept it. However, an effective vision must be attractive to build a following. The envisioned future must be per-ceived as better than where the organization is at present. People will not commit themselves to achieving a vision if it does not capture their imagi-nation and provide the excitement that is needed to overcome the inertia that exists in many firms.

Third, effective visions are shared. There is a tremendous amount of energy that is directed in a positive direction when a goal is shared. When many people within the organization co-own the vision, they put their own individual interests aside to pursue the greater goal. When people are working toward a shared long-term goal, they must communicate with one another. These discussions not only help to spread the vision, they help to create enthusiasm for it. This process helps to create a strong sense of community within the organization, and this makes it less likely that organizational subcultures will be impediments to progress.

Fourth, a clear vision also provides a much-needed unifying focus for decision makers throughout the organization. When people have a unifying focus, they tend to become more united in purpose, and there is less room for people to pursue their own individual or subgroup agendas. A compelling vision that is widely shared throughout the organization acts similarly to the way a magnet aligns iron filings: it points them in the same direction. Not only is this important in terms of getting people to work together toward a shared goal, but it also improves the day-to-day execution of strategy because decision making is consistent with the organization's vision.

Fifth, a shared vision helps to develop trust and confidence in the organization's leadership and among employees, loyalty to the organization, and positive citizenship behaviors. All of these desirable attributes promote organizational effectiveness at multiple levels.

Sixth, a successful vision is useful because it helps to define the reward system of the organization. With vision in mind, evaluation methods and compensation schemes can be developed to reward behaviors that are consonant with progress toward the vision. Conversely, behaviors that are not consonant with the vision can be identified and feedback given to help individuals and groups understand expectations. In some cases it will become clear that it is time for folks to move on because they cannot or will not commit to the direction the organization has chosen and the behaviors that support it.

Vision can also help to define the management roles and structure of the organization. Powered by a forward-looking vision, many CEOs have moved their companies to an organizational model that is flatter (fewer management levels), less formalized, and more supportive of increased levels of individual and group autonomy.

Finally, a widely shared vision promotes risk taking and experimenta-tion. Even though the end may be clear, the only way to make progress is to think "outside the box" and try new and different approaches that will move the organization forward toward the vision. Successes breed further experimentation, and failures provide additional information, which should lead to more well-informed decisions in the future.[13]

The following set of questions can serve as a checklist to make sure that an organization's vision is both well written and well conceived:

- To what extent is it future oriented?
- To what extent is it utopian (that is, likely to lead to a better future)?
- To what extent is it appropriate for the organization (that is, does it fit with its history, culture, values)?
- To what extent does it set standards of excellence and reflect high ideals?
- To what extent does it clarify purpose and direction?
- To what extent is it likely to inspire enthusiasm and encourage commitment? To what extent does it reflect uniqueness?
- Is it ambitious enough?
- To what extent is it verifiable?
- To what extent is it understandable?[14]

The Visioning Process

An effective vision rarely just comes to companies out of the blue in the form of a brilliant "eureka" flash. Visions must be developed. In this sec-tion we will outline some of the important considerations that must be kept in mind as companies develop their vision. Before delving into the process, however, one thing that should be clear is that vision is something that a company must develop for itself. Although outsiders may participate in and facilitate the process, a vision is something that must come from within. It would be both a waste of time and money to hire a consultant to come in and give the company its vision. If an organization's leaders are in-capable of creating a viable vision, the firm needs new leadership.

When it comes to developing a vision, perhaps the question most open to debate is, "Who does it?" One school of thought is that visions are developed by the organization's leader. Those subscribing to this view see the process as being top-down in nature. Maybe it is intuitively appealing to see a single charismatic leader taking the lead to create and articulate a powerful vision for the company. This approach is neat and clean, and as only one person is involved, it would most likely be internally consistent. However, the lone-wolf visioning process is very risky. If the leader is unable to craft a vision that is shared throughout the organization, it becomes useless. Moreover, the leader probably does not possess all of the knowledge that is needed to craft an effective long-term vision.

An evolution of the single-leader visioning process is one in which the process is viewed as a negotiation that takes place among a firm's top managers. Under this approach, the CEO usually takes the lead and dominates the process. The CEO presents his view of the future, including what the organization should try to become, and then tries to build a consensus around this view. The value core, then, represents the CEO's orientation and is usually not negotiable. From this starting point, other managers, either individually or in groups, negotiate on various aspects of the vision with the CEO. The hope is that in this process of give and take, managers will buy into the vision and become committed to achieving it. This view of the visioning process recognizes the social and political influences that shape the outcome.

For either of these two leader-centered processes to be effective, it is absolutely critical that the CEO champion the vision and demonstrate a commitment to making it a reality. Similarly, under these approaches, it becomes necessary to sell the idea to the rest of the organization and find ways to engage employees such that they will internalize the vision and passionately work toward its achievement.

However, another line of thinking, and one that we find more compelling—especially in terms of aligning organizational subcultures—is that the visioning process should engage many people throughout the organization. Collins makes the point that it is a waste of time trying to motivate someone because it is impossible to do. Instead, the challenge for leaders is to metaphorically "get the right people on the bus and then get the right people in the right seats."[15] The right people embrace the organization's values and are committed to moving the organization forward.

In the process of developing vision, it is important to conduct a truthful analysis of the company and the environments within which it operates. To arrive at a well-crafted vision, leaders must ask probing questions about how the organization functions. According to Collins, the essence of leadership is having the humility to admit that you may not know all the answers. Vision can be built on the answers to the right questions.

Another part of the visioning process involves the promotion of dialogue and debate. The visioning process is usually not neat, easy, orderly, or sterile. It is just the opposite, and it should involve many people who care deeply about the future of the organization and are willing to engage in intense and ongoing debate about its direction. Not only does this process give important team members a voice in the process, which is valuable, but it also gives that voice real meaning, which is crucial. The literature on participative management is fairly clear that if people participate in the process but they believe that their input was not considered, it would have been better to have never asked for their input at all. Dialogue and debate are about coming up with the answers, not about steering people toward predetermined conclusions. There is a difference, and it can be the difference between succeeding and failing in the effort.

In the visioning process, it may also be useful to bring in some key outsiders to provide additional perspectives and points of view about markets, technology, competition, and even how the organization is viewed by those outside it. This can be valuable in determining how well the organization's self-concept is being projected to other constituencies. As noted above, internal values shape the vision, but so, too, can the values and expectations of other stakeholder groups. And the closer the fit between a company's vision and the values that outside groups embrace, the better positioned the organization will be to achieve its vision.

Another thing to note about a shared visioning process is that it is iterative. A well-crafted vision isn't the result of a strictly top-down or bottom-up process; it doesn't emerge in a weekend retreat; it doesn't occur because we say it will be done by a certain date. It is an evolutionary process that, in extreme cases, may take years to develop. However, once it is complete, it should drive the organization for at least a decade. Thus, the process involves floating and debating ideas, reflecting, analyzing, revisiting, and revising them. Through the process the organization gains clarity and understanding of both the vision and the process by which it came to exist. And as those involved invest themselves in the process, a shared commitment to the outcome usually results.

In other words, a collective visioning process may lead to a more complete and well-crafted vision because it utilizes the diverse experience and perspectives of many people throughout the organization. Because the process is open and transparent, communication is improved, and this reduces the potential for organizational resistance against the vision. Furthermore, the process promotes the kind of teamwork that is important in contemporary organizations and that must be utilized to move the organization forward. However, a word of caution about the collective process is in order. A potential danger lies in the iterative process of reaching consensus: so much may have been compromised that the final product ceases to be visionary.[16]

Perhaps the most important thing to keep in mind when it comes to an organization's vision is that it must be owned by all. All organizational visions start as a personal vision held by someone, somewhere in the organization. Whether the end result emanated from the top of the organizational chart or from somewhere below is a much less important consideration than the process by which it comes to be shared. The process of developing a vision is only a small part of moving a company forward into the future and toward its potential.

How to Kill a Vision

From the discussion above, it is clear that vision is important to long-term success. Why, then, do so many organizations go through a development process only to look back and think that it was a waste of time and effort? The answer lies in the fact that visions can die for many reasons. First, vision can die if people forget that they are connected to one another. Achieving a vision requires communication, trust, and commitment to not only the vision but to one another as well. Vision is something that can be achieved only by the whole organization progressing together along the path that has been laid out. It is not the result of fits and starts by different organizational units. People generally want to be a part of a social system that binds them to something with a large and noble purpose. If they forget the connections or if the company does not reinforce them, the vision will not be realized. Only people working closely together can make it a reality.

Another reason vision dies is that people become discouraged by the lack of progress. Remember, a vision is a ten-to-thirty-year goal. Progress, especially in the beginning, is likely to be a real slog. Collins portrays this using the metaphor of a flywheel—a huge and heavy flywheel. It takes a lot of effort to get the flywheel moving, but eventually it does begin to move. The first rotation of the flywheel takes tremendous effort, but the second rotation gets a little easier, and the third easier yet. Over time the inertia becomes small, and the flywheel spins faster and faster with less and less effort. The gap between the vision and reality is large in the beginning, as the flywheel begins to move. It is the job of leaders to prevent people from becoming cynical, disheartened, or disenfranchised. With hindsight the good old days usually look better than they were. It must be made convincingly clear that the vision is sound, that it will pay off, and that going backward is not an option.

Vision can also die if the diversity of views dissipates the organization's focus on the vision. One of the biggest enemies of progress, as a vision takes hold, is organizational conflict. Conflict manifests itself in many negative ways including increased polarization, lack of trust, lack of commitment, and increased organizational politics. None of these are conducive to the type of environment that is necessary for real and sustained progress.

Vision can also die if people become so overwhelmed with the day-to-day demands of their jobs that they lose their focus on the vision. The business environment is turbulent, and the array of issues, both internal and external, with which decision makers must contend is immense. However, if people lose sight of the bigger picture and what they are trying to become, the vision becomes irrelevant.

Vision can also die when executives become impatient. We live in a society that values instant gratification. Organizational leaders are often no different (especially when their compensation is tied to short-term performance measures). Leaders must remember that vision is different from strategy. Whereas tactical moves to support a strategy can often be implemented very quickly, organizational changes to achieve a vision cannot. For many leaders, the idea of a ten-to-thirty-year goal (which may be focused on a point in time long after they retire) is antithetical to many other aspects of their jobs.

Further, vision can die from a failure of imagination. As vision is concerned with charting a new course into the future, creative thinking and problem solving become requisites for success. Without these skills, the new practices, processes, and ideas upon which a vision will be realized will not be forthcoming.

One of the most common reasons that visions die is the failure to build organization-wide consensus. The case for shared vision has been laid out at various points in this chapter. Suffice it to say that if vision isn't shared, the best one could hope for is that people accept it. However, this is not enough to make it a reality. To achieve the vision there must be a passionate commitment by the whole organization to realizing it. When it comes to vision, this is what consensus is all about.

Occasionally vision can die because of its success. Although this may sound counterintuitive, it does happen. When an organization has established a vision and then achieves it, there is a tendency to begin to drift. This is why it is important that an assessment of progress toward the vision be done on a regular and ongoing basis. As an organization approaches the realization of its vision, it must revise and extend it.

Vision can also die from a lack of flexibility. More than anything, this reflects a misunderstanding about what the vision really is. When conditions change such that the pursuit of the vision is not in the best long-term interest of the organization, leaders must be willing and able to adapt the vision to changing conditions. Although the core purpose and core values may remain constant, the long-term goal should have some basis in environmental reality.

Finally, visions can die simply from the failure to properly implement them. Remember, a vision is worth only the paper it is written on if the ideas behind it are not acted upon. Poor implementation, at any organizational level, will doom the best initiative every time.[17]

An organization composed of people at every level who understand and are passionately committed to an effective shared vision is an awesome force. Once people are committed to achieving a vision they will go to great lengths to make it happen. One of the main goals of any leader is to be worthy of his or her people. Leaders owe it to them, and to all who have a stake in a company's success, to chart a course for the future that will lead the organization to new heights. A well-conceived vision, based on an understanding of its core purpose and values, provides the organization with the direction that it must have if it is going to survive and prosper in the dynamic environment in which it competes.

Chapter Summary and Conclusions

This chapter has outlined what a vision should be and why it is critical to the success of an organization. Vision guides the organization by describing what the organization will look like in the distant future and is a motivational device for uniting the organization and moving it forward. Finally, the chapter has described how the visioning process should proceed.

Confirming Corporate Values

Over the past twenty years, management writers and practitioners have touted the importance of organizational values. However, it wasn't until Collins and Poras published *Built to Last: Successful Habits of Visionary Companies* in 1994 that the topic became mainstream.[1] Based on some of the recommendations in the book, managers, with great zeal, rushed to identify and then infuse their companies with a set of core values in the hope that these values would vault their firms to the stratosphere of corporate performance and, in the process, bestow upon these visionary leaders legendary status.

As discussed in the previous chapter, values play an important role in the establishment of a well-conceived long-term organizational vision. However, values also have a much more immediate, day-to-day impact on companies. Values shape the organization's culture, and this, in turn, affects how people interact both with each other and with important external stakeholders. These stakeholders can be customers, vendors, creditors, analysts, regulators, or any other person or group that is affected by the firm's actions. Most employees understand the importance of organizational values (and the implications of weak values) and how they are linked to the bottom line.

Research has shown that organizations with strong values (and hence strong cultures) out-performed the general stock market by a factor of 12 over a period of seventy years.[2] In another research study on the benefits of values-based culture, results indicated that workers in organizations with values-based cultures were more likely to be proud to work at their companies than those at companies that were not striving to create values-based cultures (85 percent versus 66 percent). They were also more likely to identify their companies as good places to work (80 percent versus 52 percent).[3] Unfortunately, while most companies promote a set of values, many do not live by them; as a result, the gap between what is said and what is practiced is often large.

A detailed discussion of organizational subcultures was presented in Chapters 4, 5, and 6. From this discussion it is clear that occupational, ethnic, gender, and generational differences can all impact values and behaviors at the individual level. The values that people bring with them into the workplace based on these attributes are real, and thoughtful managers need to make a genuine effort to understand them.

Subculture Constraints on Corporate Values

An influential work by Rosabeth Moss Kanter provided the cornerstone for theories about who gets ahead at work and who doesn't.[4] This work looks at how demographic attributes shape a person's experience at work and structure the distribution of roles within the organization. Kanter understood that both subcultures and organizational systems have an impact on behavior and that if organizations want to influence behavior in a certain way, they need to address the subculture dimension.[5]

At the heart of Kanter's theory is the idea that three variables—not actual demographic characteristics themselves—shape people's workplace behaviors, the nature of their interpersonal interactions, and, thus, the roles—both formal and informal—that they assume in organizations. These variables are opportunity, power, and numbers. Opportunity refers to the likelihood that someone will get ahead; power is the potential for impact that derives from a person's involvement in key activities and alliances; and numbers refers to the relative quantities of socially different people in any given setting. Kanter argues that in most organizations, opportunity and power are differentially allocated to men and women and to majorities and minorities within companies. The smaller numbers of some groups create dynamics that lead to their continued exclusion. As these dynamics are often rooted in subconscious cognitive processes, informal networks, and habitual routines, they tend to perpetuate themselves.

These insights have reframed the discussion about the existence of behaviors that conform to various subculture stereotypes. Previously it was suggested that demographically diverse individuals come into an organization with different backgrounds and varying degrees of human capital, which determine their eventual placement within the organization. Kanter's work suggests that behavior that conforms to various stereotypes is reinforced and even rewarded, which explains why some people that enter the organization with very similar credentials end up in very different power positions. Opportunity, power, and numbers play a major role both in interaction and mobility patterns.

Social identity is another mechanism that influences individual and organizational outcomes. Social identity is concerned with people's conceptions of themselves and how this, in turn, affects their behavior and interaction with others. Identity is both social (influenced by opportunity, power, and numbers) and individual. Social identity theory predicts how shared attributes and unique differences shape behavior.[6] Self-concept, then, affects the social interactions that people seek out as well as how they define the boundaries within which they construct their networks and careers.[7] Social identity theory asserts that organizational subcultures develop and reinforce behaviors, both consciously and subconsciously, due to social and individual forces.

The implications of this are both easy to see and important to address. The only way to overcome cultural constraints to organizational progress is through a set of organizational values and practices that trump those that reinforce the stereotypes of both the organization and its subcultures. Aligning organizational subcultures is concerned with breaking down those things that reinforce subculture stereotypes by implementing a set of "hypervalues" and organizational practices that supersede those of various subcultures.

The Concept of Hypervalues

The term hypervalues refers to a set of organizational values that represent principles or philosophies that are fundamental to the organization's success. These values are seen as crucial to building an organization's self-concept, business philosophy, and desired external image—all of which have been linked to high organizational performance. Thus, hypervalues represent what are generally referred to as "core values," but it also implies something more: these values supersede any value or set of values that may be held by organizational subcultures. Hypervalues define what the organization is all about, and they detail those things that are nonnegotiable in the conduct of business. In fact, these values are so important that they would continue to be held even if they became a business impediment. Hypervalues are universal in nature. That is, they are not limited to any organizational subculture but apply universally across all organizational units and to every aspect of a firm's activities.

In cases where hypervalues conflict with those of a subculture, the hypervalues must be applied. If they are not, then they are not true hypervalues. In those situations where a hypervalue is not violated, subcultural values may shape attitudes, behaviors, and decisions. However, if decision makers evaluate the appropriateness of an action by comparing it with subcultural norms, then the appropriateness of the action depends only on the values of the subculture. In some matters this may be acceptable, but in others it can cause problems. The important thing to note is that under no circumstance should a behavior, action, or decision violate a hypervalue.

In companies with weak organizational culture there is usually a weakly enforced, or nonexistent, set of core values. In these companies there is usually a good deal of chaos, confusion, and conflict. As different subcultures apply their own standards in making decisions, there is no common framework that decision makers throughout the organization can follow. In contrast, companies with a strong corporate culture have a strongly enforced set of hypervalues. Employees throughout these companies know what is vitally important to the organization's success and what it is that the company holds dear. These values are not open to debate. They serve as clear, defining principles by which the firm conducts itself in both the present and future. In companies with strong organizational culture, employees follow subcultural values only when a hypervalue is not being violated. However, hypervalues supersede, and invalidate, inconsistent subcultural norms.

National context or national culture presents perhaps the greatest challenge to a company's hypervalues, but even these must not trump a company's core beliefs. For example, in some countries, women are assigned a lower status than men in the social order. If a company has a hypervalue based on the idea of fairness, then fairness in all aspects of business activities must be enforced. Making an exception in a country with different cultural values is unacceptable. If a company cannot or will not enforce this value in all cases, it is simply not a core value.

Signs of Trouble in a Weak Corporate Culture

Research has consistently demonstrated the importance of a strong corporate culture for companies. As discussed above, core values are the bedrock of a strong corporate culture. But how does a leader know whether his organization has a weak culture—one that needs to be changed? The answer lies in the fact that companies with weak culture usually exhibit several warning signs, including the following:

- There are no clear values or beliefs about how to succeed in their competitive environments; or there are many such beliefs but a lack of agreement among organizational members about which ones are most important; or different parts of the company have fundamentally different beliefs.
- The heroes of the culture are destructive or disruptive and don't build any common understanding about what is important.
- The rituals and day-to-day life are either disorganized or contradictory.
- The company has an inward, not outward, focus. Too much attention is devoted to internal politics and not enough on market realities and achieving competitive advantage.
- The company has a short-term focus, with activities centered on immediate performance and not on developing enduring and sustainable businesses.
- Morale is low, and people are unhappy working for the firm. Turnover is high, and positive values are not transferred to newly hired workers or reinforced among existing workers.
- Fragmentation and inconsistency are the order of the day, and as a result, people do not (and generally don't even make an effort to)

understand one another. Differences are reinforced, and therefore motivation and performance decline.

- Confusion and frustration result in frequent emotional outbursts, as employees become anxious and confused by ambiguity and mixed messages.
- Subcultures become ingrown, and there is little or no attempt to work or communicate across organizational units.
- Subcultures try to undermine each other in an attempt to gain political clout and increase their individual power base.
- Subcultures become exclusive and arbitrarily limit membership and interaction with the subgroup. Exclusivity places the interests of the subgroup over the interests of the larger organization.
- Subculture values preempt company values and, as a result, no common shared set of values can exist.[8]
- Arrogance leads managers to believe that they have all the answers and don't need organizational input to make difficult and complex decisions.
- The organization is hostile to leadership and other drivers of change. As the environment becomes more turbulent, adherence to the status quo is not a viable option, and organizations that promote stability over adaptation are likely to become increasingly marginalized.[9]

Managers must be aware of these potential problems and be prepared to address them at the earliest sign that they are beginning to develop. Corporate culture is too fragile to be left unmanaged. Only leaders that keep their finger on the pulse of the organization, including its subcultures, will be in a position to nurture a strong and shared set of values that will promote a strong and viable corporate culture.

Understanding the Corporate Culture–Values Link

Corporate culture is inherently complex, but it has been widely recognized as a resource that can provide a sustainable source of competitive advantage when it is strong. A strong corporate culture can have powerful consequences. It can enable a company to take decisive action to achieve organizational objectives or to respond to a crisis or changing market conditions; or it can cause a group of bright folks to walk hand in hand over a cliff. An expert on corporate culture has provided a useful framework for understanding the link between corporate culture and values.[10] The framework can be visualized as a series of concentric rings that represent different levels of corporate culture. Working from the outer ring toward the center, the levels of culture are artifacts, behaviors, espoused values, and core values. Each of these levels has an impact on corporate culture and, as such, must be understood and aligned with the other levels. As one progresses from the outer level (artifacts) to the center (core values), the properties of the levels become more difficult to observe. In other words, one can see cultural artifacts very easily, whereas core values are held subconsciously and thus are very difficult to observe.

Artifacts are those elements of culture that are easily observed and relatively superficial. Artifacts are the physical manifestations of the culture, including organizational structures, rules, processes, physical layout and other physical characteristics, status symbols, company rites and rituals, and attire. Artifacts also include the things people talk about on a daily basis and the positions they take in these discussions. Artifacts are usually rooted in deeper aspects of the culture.

Behaviors are the pattern of actions that are considered normal and acceptable within an organization. Although behaviors are not usually prescribed in company materials, they are often considered the informal, or unwritten, rules that govern conduct. Behaviors are not as visible as artifacts, but they can be observed. They are often clear to insiders, and astute outsiders can understand them as well. Because behaviors are heavily influenced by values, the identification and understanding of behaviors are necessary precursors to understanding values at a deeper level.

Espoused values are the values that an organization claims to hold. These values can be developed to provide direction or as a matter of practicality but they are not necessarily (and often are not) deeply held or widely shared. As such, they may or may not be central to an organization's corporate culture—at least not in its current form. When values are espoused but not widely embraced, they really have a minimal impact on the organization's true corporate culture. And if an espoused value is not widely held throughout the organization, it will generally have very little impact on behaviors, although it may have a negative impact on attitudes—especially those that deal with confidence and trust in the organization's leadership.

Core values are the widely shared beliefs within the organization that are assumed or taken for granted. Core values are often subconsciously held values that really define what an organization is all about. These values are enduring over time, and they comprise a set of ideas that the organization considers non-negotiable and indispensable. Sometimes core values are so fundamental that they are not even consciously considered. Organizations with a strong culture have a set of core values that shapes behaviors on a daily basis, although employees may have trouble putting it into words. Organizations with a weak corporate culture may have subcultures within the organization with their own sets of values that are stronger than anything that exists organization-wide. In these cases, a lack of core values contributes to chaos, confusion, and conflict.

Because culture manifests itself at different levels, an approach to cultural change that is profound and long lasting must be implemented on several fronts. Although it might be relatively easy to change cultural artifacts, these changes are generally superficial and unlikely to have a lasting impact on behaviors. A change in behaviors is more difficult to produce, but it can be done. However, changing behavior in a consistent way across an organization is undoubtedly a challenge. Once a behavior is changed, it can reasonably be expected that the change will have some staying power. Core values, the bedrock of corporate culture, are often very difficult to change. As they are deeply held, a sound rationale for their change must be provided. However, it should be understood that changing core values does not happen quickly; it can take years to accomplish.

For leaders, the implications of this framework should be clear. Before any attempt at change is initiated, leaders should understand the following:

- In order to change core values leaders must have a thorough understanding of what values are currently considered core (or be able to verify that no core values exist). The starting point of any intervention is a thorough understanding of the status quo.

- A set of desired core values must be identified, and leaders must make it clear that these values are important and central to everything that the organization does. In addition, leaders must present a compelling business case for why a given set of core values is necessary and how embracing these values will benefit the organization in the long term.
- Communication of the core values must be thorough, constant, and conducted primarily by senior leadership. (Communication of core values is discussed in more detail in Chapter 10.)
- Artifacts must be aligned with the desired values by changing organizational processes, evaluation and compensation systems, organizational structure, facilities layout, and so on. Business artifacts must support the desired culture.
- Efforts must be taken to reinforce desirable behaviors that reflect the core values so that they become the norm. This must be done through artifacts that include recognition, rewards, feedback, and so on.
- Leaders must model the desired values. A top-down approach is the only way that values initiatives will succeed, and leaders must be relentless in promoting the core values.

These efforts should help companies to develop a set of core values that results in a strong corporate culture and the many benefits that a strong corporate culture provides. Organizations that have a strong corporate culture are characterized by leaders and lower-level employees that share the same values and hold the same priorities. There is no ambiguity about what is vitally important to the success of the firm. Moreover, in organizations with a strong corporate culture, the values are lived on a daily basis and, as a result, new employees usually pick them up very quickly. In such organizations, a relatively new executive is just as likely to be corrected by subordinates as by superiors for a violation of cultural norms. The values upon which strong corporate cultures are built tend not to change much when a new CEO takes charge, because they run so deep.

It has been suggested that strong corporate cultures encourage performance for several reasons. First, the alignment of goals across organizational units assures that people are working toward the same ends and not at cross-purposes. Second, they help create and maintain high levels of motivation throughout the firm. And, finally, strong corporate cultures positively impact performance because they provide sufficient structure and controls without relying on stifling bureaucracy.[11]

In the final analysis, the contention that strong corporate cultures and performance are positively related is not controversial. Similarly, the link between values and corporate culture is not in dispute. For companies to realize their potential, they must identify and embrace a set of values that fundamentally shape the way business is conducted on a day-to-day basis by providing guidance to decision makers throughout the firm on the many complex decisions that must be made.

Core Values—More than Words

Core values are meaningless if they are not universally accepted and embraced across all organizational units. Let's take a company with the following core values: communication, respect, integrity, excellence. Who could disagree with this set of values? The images these words evoke are some of the strongest and most positive that can be imagined. The company that boldly proclaimed these values in their 2000 annual report was Enron. This company is now one of the most disgraced in U.S. history. Enron's downfall did not result because their values were bad. Their downfall happened because, at least for a small number of people in positions of power, their values were merely empty words. The point to remember is that unless values are shared and embraced by all organizational subcultures, they are meaningless. Or, even worse, they may have negative impacts on the organization.

Empty values statements often create cynical and dispirited employees, alienate customers and vendors, and generally undermine managerial credibility. When a company promotes a set of values and then operates in a manner that is inconsistent with the values, all of these can, and probably will, occur. Today, around 80 percent of the Fortune 100 companies publicly promote their values. This effort is clearly aimed at influencing not only employees but external stakeholders as well. It is easy to determine which companies mean what they say and which companies use espoused values as "window dressing."

Core values that are lived can separate a company from all others. Values can provide a unique, identifying stamp that is not easy for competitors to copy. However, even though strong values can result in multiple positive outcomes, they are not easily attained. In fact, when practiced, values can cause real pain for an organization in the following ways:

- Employees that fail to embrace the values often feel like outcasts. It is probably not realistic to expect these folks to give their all for the good of the cause when they don't believe in the cause.
- Values can limit an organization's strategic and operational freedom. In some cases, market opportunities, or options for operating efficiencies, may need to be passed over if they do not fit with the company's values.
- Values constrain employee behavior. Although this promotes consistency, some people may feel too tied down or too limited in their ability to creatively solve problems.
- Strongly shared values leave executives open to criticism for even minor violations of the values. When organizational values are promoted they must apply to everyone equally—no exceptions. Employees look to executives to model the values to the letter of the law.
- Values demand constant vigilance. There are no days off or looking the other way when it comes to values enforcement. Passes such as these send the message that the values are really dispensable.[12]

The bottom line is that if you are not prepared to deal with the pain, it is probably better to not go through the charade of developing and promoting core values in the first place. Once they are made public, the values set a transparent standard for behavior and decision making. To be meaningful, values must exhibit the following characteristics:

- They are shared by everyone in the organization.
- They state what is authentically believed.
- They guide day-to-day work behaviors.
- They are fully integrated into the business strategy, organizational processes, and daily organizational decisions.[13]

Types of Values

Much confusion in the discussion on values stems from the fact that the terminology is imprecise. Not all values are the same, and the use of one term to describe different concepts muddies the waters. We believe that precisely defining different types of values aids in both discussion and understanding. One framework that addresses this problem identifies four different types of values:

- *Core values*, as stated previously, are deeply ingrained principles upon which an organization's culture is built. An organization's success is dependent on its core values. Core values can be actively developed and nurtured, but they often originate with the founding of the company. In other cases, they emerge as a result of the way a crisis or situation has been handled. Core values are the guiding principles that should be held even if they become a business impediment.
- *Aspirational values* are those that a company does not currently possess but needs to develop in the future. An aspirational value is one that a company develops to address changing environmental conditions. An aspirational value is one that would be added to the core; it does not dilute core values.
- *Permission-to-play values* are social and behavioral guidelines that all employees must follow. These values can be viewed as expectations that often exist across companies. Examples might include honesty, integrity, truthfulness, timeliness, and so on. These values don't differentiate one company from another, but they do outline the basic expectations of all employees who work for the organization.
- *Accidental values* are those that develop over time. These values are norms that the company and its employees accept as a normal way of doing business. Although accidental values may become ingrained over time, a company's leadership team must be aware of the emergence of these values and determine whether they are an asset or whether they threaten the core.[14]

As mentioned in the previous chapter, part of establishing a viable long-term vision involves a determination of a company's core values. Collins and Poras make the point that core values require no external justification (although they can convey important information to external stakeholders). Core values have intrinsic value in and of themselves, and they are extremely important to employees.[15]

Further, contemporary thinking on core values suggests that it is far less important to identify the "right" set of core values than it is for companies to have some set of values that they truly own. For example, a company need not have customer service as a core value (Sony doesn't) or respect for the individual (Disney doesn't) or quality (Wal-Mart doesn't) or teamwork (Nordstrom doesn't).[16] Although a company may have operating practices that support customer service or respect or quality or teamwork, that does not mean that these practices are at its core. For companies the message is simple: identify a set of values that can be considered core because they help promote a business philosophy and culture that leads to sustainable competitive advantage and then passionately drive them home. There is no right answer, but when a company identifies and reinforces a set of values, they need to do so with great conviction.

When it comes to identifying a set of core values, most companies opt to go with three to five values. As mentioned previously, these are the small number of things that a company considers so fundamental that they will stand the test of time. An important thing to remember is that core values need to be authentic; you can't fake them. People both inside and outside the organization will easily be able to tell when a company is merely going through the motions—either because there is no commitment to the espoused values or, worse, actions conflict with the values.

When a company does not currently hold any core values, subcultural norms can create chaos and confusion. So how does a company go about developing them? First, they need to look inside to see if there are any values that are currently embraced. If the answer is "no," it is up to the organization's leaders to identify some. Although visioning may be an exercise that involves people throughout the organization, the identification and reinforcement of core values should be a more tightly controlled process. The top leadership team must take the central role in developing core values.

It is important to understand that when a company develops its values, the goal isn't consensus. Involving a broad group made up of folks throughout the organization to determine the organization's values is a bad idea for a couple of reasons. First, it gives the impression that all input is equally valuable. In addition, it incorporates the suggestions of many people that probably don't positively contribute to the organization.[17] Taken together, these conditions would likely yield a set of values that are confused and contradictory and that appeal to the lowest common denominator. Core values should reflect what is best about the company.

It may be very difficult, or even unreasonable, to expect disinterested employees to buy into a set of values. The important task for leadership is to identify individuals that are predisposed to embrace them and to make sure that these people are retained and those with similar inclinations are drawn to the organization. Those who cannot, or will not, buy into the values need to go elsewhere. A company simply cannot operate effectively when there are people working at cross-purposes with one another. Requiring the acceptance of core values does not mean that an organization is promoting a homogenous workforce—quite the contrary. Companies need to understand that a diversity of people leads to a diversity of ideas about how to creatively solve problems and effectively move the organization forward. One thing that employees must share, however, is a fundamental belief in a set of values about how the organization does business which is not dispensable when the going gets tough.

Jack Welch understood these principles as he remade GE into a world-class company. In GE's 1991 annual report, Welch outlined the importance of values and how important they were when he defined four types of executives:

The first is one who delivers on commitments—financial or otherwise—and shares the values of our Company. His or her future is an easy call. Onward and upward.

The second type of leader is one who does not meet commitments and does not share our values. Not as pleasant a call, but equally as easy.

The third is one who misses commitments but shares the values. He or she usually gets a second chance, preferably in a different environment.

Then there's the fourth type—the most difficult for many of us to deal with. That leader delivers on commitments, makes all the numbers, but doesn't share the values we must have. This is the individual who typically forces performance out of people rather than inspires it: the autocrat, the big shot, the tyrant. Too often all of us have looked the other way—tolerated these "type 4" managers because "they always deliver"—at least in the short term.

And perhaps this type was more acceptable in easier times, but in an environment where we must have every good idea from every man and woman in the organization, we cannot afford management styles that suppress and intimidate. Whether we can convince and help these managers to change—recognizing how difficult that can be—or part company with them if they cannot, will be the ultimate test of our commitment to the transformation of this Company and will determine the future of the mutual respect and trust we are building. . . . We know now that without leaders who "walk the talk," all of our plans, promises, and dreams for the future are just that—talk.

Determining Core Values

A number of things are important to keep in mind when it comes to determining a company's core values. First, leadership at the top of the organization needs to own the process. This is simply too important to hand off to an organizational unit or to hope that values will just bubble up from lower levels in the organization. Ideally, the CEO, any founders that are still with the company, and a handful of key employees (usually from the executive team) should be involved.

A second consideration is that the values process should be given enough time so that decision makers get it right. Companies arrive at their core values through a process. It is better for the values team to arrive at a workable set of values than to rush to decide on a set of values that it might later regret. Part of the process should allow for a period of time for the leadership team to reflect upon a draft set of values to ensure that they truly do fit the organization—both now and in the plausible future. If an organization has operating units in other countries, they must also make sure that the values translate as intended across national borders.

One final thought about values in is order. We don't want to leave the impression that values last forever. The above notwithstanding, leaders must understand that as conditions change, a change in values may be necessary to create a necessary degree of fit between the company and the new situation. Values become ingrained with organizational success, but when the rules for success change, so do the underlying means to be successful. Some external changes that have forced companies to re-evaluate their business models, including a rethinking about which values allow them to be successful, are deregulation, the emergence of high customer expectations, dynamic competition, increasing rates of innovation, and opportunities presented by globalization, to name a few.

Values generally do not change quickly, especially if they are strong and operate at the subconscious level. And in response to a change, a company does not need to abandon the whole value set. It may be necessary to rethink one or two values or perhaps add a value to the existing set. The point is that although values are enduring, when the business environment changes in such a way that holding (or failing to hold) an existing value or set of values threatens the viability of the organization, everything is fair game.

Even a company like Hewlett-Packard, which for decades embraced a value of respect for employees, has been forced to lay off workers and adopt new human resource practices using temporary workers. Throughout the change process, the most important determinant of success is competent leadership at the top of the organization. Leaders are able to identify a set of core values, make the business case for their importance, and then develop and energize key groups of insiders to help make the change happen.

Chapter Summary and Conclusions

Leaders throughout the firm must understand and appreciate the role that values play in organizational success. Subcultures within companies develop and reinforce behaviors, both consciously and subconsciously, due to a variety of social and individual forces. To be effective, organizational values must be stronger than those of any and all subcultures. These values, referred to as hypervalues, can be seen as a way to guard against excessive reliance on subcultural values. When subcultural values conflict with hypervalues, the latter must dominate. Although subcultural values may shape attitudes, behaviors, and decisions, they must remain subordinate to hypervalues for a strong positive corporate culture to develop and be sustained.

A strong corporate culture, in which a shared set of core values guides behavior and decision making throughout the organization, is positively related to organizational performance. A weak corporate culture is associated with confusion, chaos, and conflict. Managers must be aware of signs of trouble in a company with a weak culture because the result is likely to be poor performance and a troublesome work environment. The ability to spot and address problems before they affect performance, or to solve problems that are currently affecting performance, allows a company to make progress toward sustainable competitive advantage.

The link between corporate culture and values is clear, and it is difficult to discuss one without the other. Managers must understand this connection and work to align the various dimensions of corporate culture. Strong, shared core values are the bedrock of corporate culture. For core values to have a positive impact on organizations they must be universally accepted and embraced across all organizational units. The values must be authentic, and they must apply to everyone. While living a set of core values may be painful at times, the end result is worth it.

Contemporary thinking suggests that there is no such thing as a universal set of "right" values for all companies. It is important that companies identify a set of values and work to instill these values throughout the organization. The process of determining core values must be driven by top leadership and then actively championed by them. However, once internalized, values tend to perpetuate themselves as they are formally communicated; used in recruitment, hiring, orientation, and evaluation processes; modeled by those in leadership positions; reinforced through company rites and rituals; and spread to new workers through mentoring programs. While core values have enduring properties, they can be changed or revised if conditions warrant.

Communicating Vision and Values

Business strategists are in agreement that organizations in which major corporate culture change has taken place successfully tend to have the following characteristics in common:

- The CEO and other top managers had a strategic vision of what the organization could become and communicated this vision to employees at all levels.
- The vision was translated into the key measures designed to accomplish that vision. These measures were communicated widely through contests, formal and informal recognition, and monetary rewards, among other devices.[1]

Similarly, in his book on leadership, Max DePree describes the important role of communicating values in the success of organizations:

An increasingly large part that communication plays in expanding [corporate] cultures is to pass along values to new [organizational] members and reaffirm those values to old hands. A corporation's values are its life's blood. Without effective communication, actively practiced, with the art of scrutiny, those values will disappear in a sea of trivial memos and impertinent reports.[2]

The leadership in many, if not most, organizations has been trained to communicate in a rational, logical manner that is rife with numbers and other quantitative support. However, the message suggested by the above excerpts is that to make the strategic change process effective, those leading the process must enlist methods of communication and rhetoric that are designed to inspire employees throughout the organization. Moreover, communication that also appeals to employees' emotions rather than simply to logic has been found to more effective.

In the next few sections of this chapter we focus on some techniques that you can use to more effectively communicate vision and values to employees. Once we have explained each of these techniques, we turn our attention to how they might be applied as vision and values are communicated to specific organizational subcultures.

Techniques for Communicating Vision and Values

A number of communication and rhetorical techniques have been identified for effectively communicating vision.[3] These techniques include the following:

- *Simplicity:* All jargon and "techno babble" must be eliminated.
- *Metaphor, analogy, and example:* A verbal picture is worth a thousand words.
- *Multiple forums:* Big meetings and small, memos and newspapers, formal and informal interaction—all are effective for spreading the word.
- *Repetition:* Ideas sink in deeply only after they have been heard many times.
- *Leadership by example:* Behavior from important people that is inconsistent with the vision overwhelms other forms of communication.
- *Explanation of seeming inconsistencies:* Unaddressed inconsistencies undermine the credibility of all communication.
- *Give-and-take.* Two-way communication is always more powerful than one-way communication.

All of these techniques are equally applicable to communicating values as well as vision. In the following section, we address each one of these techniques using illustrative examples and introduce two additional techniques not included in this list.

Keep It Simple

The term slang has been defined as an expression, often short-lived, that is identified with a specific group of people.[4] Using appropriate slang in everyday speech presents no communication problem; it can convey precise information and often indicates group membership. However, the use of slang creates a communication problem when the sender uses a slang term that the person receiving the message does not understand.

Many business disciplines have slang words and jargon that are easily understood by colleagues in the same discipline. For example, if you are directing your communications to a group of marketing managers, acronyms such as CRM (for customer relationship management) might be appropriate because the communicator can safely assume that the managers will immediately understand its meaning. However, when attempting to communicate vision to diverse groups of organizational subcultures, it is not wise to use slang and jargon. It is always wise to stay away from these communication shortcuts when you want to make sure everyone fully understands what you are communicating to them.

Use Metaphors and Analogies

It has been suggested that inspiring leaders use a number of rhetorical techniques such as metaphors, analogies, different language styles, and rhythmic devices to ensure that the symbolic content of their communication has a profound impact on those receiving the communication.[5] The reasoning is that metaphors and analogies juxtapose similarities between two things that can often be quite different.

Their purpose is to stimulate the various senses of the audience and simultaneously create a vivid and memorable experience. As listeners (for example, members of organizational subcultures) of the communication decipher its meaning, they pay closer attention to what is being said.[6] This causes visual, cognitive, and emotional responses as they apply the decoded communications to their experiences.[7] The result is that a leader's words often make their greatest impact as symbols rather than as literal meanings.

Lee Iacocca, longtime CEO of Chrysler, used this technique very effectively. For example, in explaining a decision to cut his salary to one dollar, he employed the metaphor of a military commander joining his troops in the trenches. He was first cited as saying, "I didn't take one dollar a year to be a martyr, I took it because I had to go into the pits." He then extended the analogy to the family, stating: "I call this equality of sacrifice. . . . It wasn't the loans that saved us, although we needed them badly. It was the hundreds of millions of dollars given up by everybody involved."[8]

He implied in this analogy that he and his fellow Chrysler workers were all members of a common family working hard to prove their worth. By invoking this analogy of family, he attempted to create strong identification between himself and the average Chrysler worker. He interpreted the hardships that Chrysler employees experienced as necessary for the well-being of the "family." This rhetorical tactic effectively engaged the emotions of Chrysler employees by associating the Chrysler situation with traditional family values. By tying the company crisis to a positive analogy, employees were provided with a rationale for their difficulties.

Why does this technique work so well to communicate vision? Research from the field of speech communication shows that metaphors and analogies appear to excite the imagination of the listener and create consecutive states of tension and tension release.[9] The rationale is that the listener is not a passive listener; rather these techniques trigger a state of active thinking as listeners puzzle over the meaning of the metaphor or analogy and attempt to make sense of it in light of their own situation.

Moreover, in the field of social psychology, studies show that these rhetorical devices are a more persuasive and effective means of communicating ideas. It has been found that using statistical data to convey information is viewed as uninformative. On the other hand, brief face-to-face comments using this technique offer more vivid information. It may be concluded that information is used in proportion to its "vividness."[10] Communicating vision is critical to the effectiveness of the strategic change approach. The use of metaphors and analogies in communicating vision helps to ensure that it is understood and accepted by organizational subcultures.

Use Multiple Forums

For the most part, the CEO communicates the vision and values to organizational members. Annual meetings usually provide the forum for this communication. The communication may then be repeated in smaller departmental meetings to reinforce the values and by individual managers seeking the support of their employees in implementing various aspects of the vision in the tasks assigned to their particular department.

Often the vision and some of the values are displayed in large signs or placards in prominent areas of the organization. One example that comes to mind is Whole Foods Corporation, a large natural foods grocer headquartered in Austin, Texas. In each of the company's stores, the vision and values are painted on the wall near the cash registers. This is viewed as one forum to communicate vision and values to employees as they go about their tasks, as well as to customers as they wait in line to pay for their groceries.

In addition to this forum, many companies have their vision and values printed on plaques, key chains, coffee cups, or some other personal items that are given to employees. These items are seen or used daily by employees and serve as a constant reminder of the purpose of the organization. The more alternative forums are used, the greater the chance that employees will remember and embrace the vision and values.

Use Repetition

While the use of multiple forums can be considered a form of repetition, other forms can also be employed to emphasize the vision and values of the organization. For example, within the realm of rhetoric, several techniques involving repetition of words, rhythm, balance, and alliteration can be employed to solidify the message being communicated to employees. Although politicians and clergy are typical users of these techniques, leadership within organizations can also use these techniques effectively to communicate vision and values to organizational subcultures.

Within the realm of politics, it has been found that a certain rhythm can be mesmerizing to an audience.[11] President Franklin Roosevelt often employed alliteration (that is, the repetition of initial consonant sounds in two or more neighboring words or syllables). An example of this is when Roosevelt was describing leadership during the depression: "Those who tilled the soil no longer reaped the rewards which were their right. The small measure of their gains was decreed by men in distant cities. . . . Individual initiative was crushed in the cogs of a great machine." The message was heightened by alliteration, as shown by the repeated initial letters in this passage (r, r, r, d, d, i, i, c, c). This creates an alliteration-holding rhythm.

Dr. Martin Luther King Jr., who demonstrated the mastery of repetition and rhythm in his "I have a dream" speech, provides another example:

> So let freedom ring from the prodigious hilltops of New Hampshire. Let freedom ring from the mighty mountains of New York. Let freedom ring from the snow-capped Rockies of Colorado. Let freedom ring from the curvaceous slopes of California. But not only that. Let freedom ring from Stone Mountain of Georgia. Let freedom ring from Lookout Mountain of Tennessee. Let freedom ring from every hill and molehill of Mississippi, from every mountainside, let freedom ring. And when we allow freedom to ring, when we let it ring from every village and hamlet, from every state and city, we will be able to speed up that day when all of God's children—black men and white men, Jews and Gentiles, Catholics and Protestants—will be able to join hands and sing in the words of the old Negro spiritual. Free at last, free at last, thank God Almighty, we are free at last.[12]

Dr. King used the phrase "let freedom ring" over and over as he increased his tone, closing with the repeated phrase "free at last." The repetition and rhythm impacted the listening audience in two important ways. First, Dr. King was able to capture the attention and mesmerize the audience with the song-like crescendo, and second and more importantly, he was able to leave the audience with one critical idea, "they are to be free." The repetition ensured recall. The spoken message is more difficult to comprehend because once the communicator speaks the words they are gone; but repetition helps the audience recall important ideas.[13]

If an idea is paramount to the vision or values of your organization, the use of repetition, rhythm, and alliteration can help communicate its importance and ensure that employees remember it.

Lead by Example

The old saying, "a picture is worth a thousand words" captures the concept of leading by example quite well. A leader can profess a value such as honor or integrity to the organization, but if the leader does not model these values, employees cannot be expected to accept and embrace these values. Many leaders are gifted orators; however, if a leader's actions do not model what he is professing, employees soon realize that he is "talking the talk but not walking the talk." As a result, employees ignore what the leader has to say.

We believe that leading by example is the most important way to communicate an organization's vision and values. If organizational leaders believe that a set of values is crucial for the success of the organization but they are not willing to model those values in their actions, they might as well give up and accept defeat.

Leaders in some organizations may communicate the message that high-quality products or services are important to the organization and then implement low-cost strategies on purchased parts or cut the training budget for new hires. What message is sent by these actions? Likewise, some leaders may communicate verbally that they value personal integrity. Those words are lost on employees if they later see those same leaders accepting gifts from vendors in return for buying their products, when it is known that another product is better.

No matter how well vision and values are communicated, the leadership communicating them must be willing to live that vision and model those values for the message to be accepted and embraced by employees of the various organizational subcultures.

Explain Inconsistencies

If it has been communicated to employees that the quality of the organization's products is critical to organizational success and then a low-cost purchasing strategy is implemented, there must be a good explanation for this action, since it is inconsistent with the message that was communicated. When vision and values are communicated to employees, words and deeds must be examined for any inconsistencies.

As discussed earlier, inconsistencies can be interpreted as not "walking the talk" and may result in an undermining of the values communicated to employees. When employees are required to act in ways that seem inconsistent with an organization's vision and values, a rationale for these actions must be provided so that employees can reconcile the apparent contradiction between these actions and the organization's communicated vision and values.

For example, a low-cost strategy may be needed for only a short period of time because of short-term cash flow problems. Consistent with the organization's values, new quality assurance methods might be instituted to ensure that overall quality is maintained in spite of using a low-cost part provider. This rationale must be communicated to employees to help them see that their actions are not counter to the communicated vision and values, even though they may appear that way.

Encourage Two-Way Communications

Organizational leaders may find themselves falling into a pattern of one-way communication. They communicate what should be done, and employees are expected to do it. However, employees may have valuable insights into how vision and values can be operationalized within the context of the organization. The lessons learned from reengineering, continuous improvement, and other business improvement concepts tell us that employees have valuable input to any decision made within their business units. Furthermore, when communicating vision and values, employees of the various organizational subcultures are more likely to accept and support them if they are involved to some extent in the process.

Frame Your Communications

A technique not included in the list presented at the beginning of this section is framing. Research on transformational leadership suggests that crafting and communicating an inspirational vision is critical for the success of the organization.[14] The manner in which a leader describes the future of his or her organization is in essence the vision. A leader can say, "I want us to build 100,000 new computers next year with a 15 percent return on assets," or "I want us to revolutionize how people work in the global economy through the use of our product." Both statements define a vision for the organization, but each has a different meaning.

Both statements offer distinct ways of "framing" an organization's strategic vision. The first is framed around quantitative measures; the second offers a grand purpose. Frames offer a snapshot of organizations at a point in time and provide a road map for action. Sailors who believed the earth was round were eager to sail toward the horizon ahead because they knew there was unexplored territory beyond that horizon. Similarly, if leaders believe that their organization is "round" rather than "flat," they will frame their organization's reality based on that perspective.

In one research study, participants were told that a project had an 80 percent chance of success and that another project had a 20 percent chance of failure.[15] When participants were asked to select a project, they overwhelmingly chose the first one over the second, even though both had exactly the same success rate and failure rate. Effective framing of the organizational vision helps to build a sense of confidence and excitement about the future. Leaders must communicate using positive and inspiring frames if they want employees to be motivated by the vision they are promoting.

Use Stories to Communicate Values

Another technique not included in the list is using stories to illustrate values. The following story provides a great example of this technique:

> An MBA candidate was being recruited by a firm. At the end of a day of interviews, he had met with everyone except the company's charismatic president.

Up until this point, there was a clear consensus that the young man should be hired. At 5:30 P.M., he met with the president who promptly asked if he would join him with another manager for drinks. Off they went to a nearby bar, at which point the president called his wife and the wife of the manager to join them for dinner.

The MBA proceeded off to dinner, having yet to begin his interview with the president. Dinner ended at midnight—still no interview had been conducted. The president then asked the recruit to his home for the actual interview. The young man balked with surprise, saying he was tired and needed to return home. Needless to say, he was not offered the position.[16]

The company president and others repeated this story often to illustrate that the organization's mission demanded a willingness to "roll with the punches" and "to go the extra mile." The story was a far more powerful and vivid means of illustrating what the leader saw as important values and behaviors than simple statements that employees should be willing to demonstrate greater commitment. Because values often imply actions and behaviors, it is important to use techniques such as stories to illustrate these rather abstract concepts. Stories help the reader comprehend these concepts in concrete terms.

Another related concept is the use of stories that incorporate symbols that have strong cultural roots. An example is the story of David and Goliath, which can be used to illustrate a small, brave company or individual going up against a giant corporation or opponent and winning. The device of stories can be used effectively to communicate and model organizational values. Leaders should utilize stories and symbols whenever possible to help members of organizational subcultures visualize the values of the organization.

Modifying Communication Techniques for Organizational Subcultures

If we could be sure that everyone had the same perceptions and understanding of what we say, it would be much easier to communicate. However, one communications expert suggests that each person has a unique perception of reality based on his or her individual experiences, culture, emotions at the moment, knowledge, socioeconomic status, and a host of other variables.[17]

All of these variables together act as a filter. That is, as organization members receive messages, they begin to interpret those messages, through their filters, to make meaning out of what they hear. If the message is consistent with their existing beliefs, it is more likely to create a lasting impression and generate a stronger response than messages that are counter to their beliefs.[18]

It is not surprising that members of various organizational subcultures possess filters that affect how they understand and subsequently align themselves with the vision and values communicated to them. Some of the filters relate to those traits that separate them into the various subcultures. When attempts are made to align each of the subcultures with the vision and values of the organization, leaders must modify their message so that they can overcome the barriers some of these filters create. In the next few sections of this chapter, we discuss the filters that may exist within various subcultures and suggest techniques to overcome the barriers these filters may be creating.

Occupational Subcultures

As mentioned earlier, jargon generally should not be used when communicating vision and values. A problem arises when slang or jargon is not uniformly understood among all those who hear it. Nevertheless, when addressing specific occupational groups, such as engineers for instance, jargon may be appropriate. Many occupations, particularly the more technical ones, have their own jargon. That jargon frequently provides a very efficient way to communicate to that specific group.

Furthermore, the use of appropriate jargon often helps listeners feel that the person speaking identifies with and understands them. They accept the speaker as "one of us." Moreover, this identification helps the message penetrate the filters members of a specific occupation may have. However, when using specific jargon, it is imperative that it be used correctly and that it be used to address only this select group. This often necessitates delivering different messages to different occupational subcultures. The payoff for this extra effort is increased alignment of this subculture with the overall vision and values of the organization.

Another strategy that can be employed with occupational subcultures is to have "one of their own" communicate organizational vision and values to them. Occupational subcultures often have greater respect and cohesion with individuals who possess the same skills and certifications. For example, when a staff person such as a departmental secretary disseminates, via email, a college-wide policy that affects only professors, professors may ignore the policy because they feel that a secretary should not be directing their actions, even though the secretary did not create the policy. In contrast, if the department chair communicates the same information, it will be probably be accepted immediately. Employing a member of the occupational subculture as a spokesperson can be an effective way to help occupational subcultures to align more closely with the corporate culture of the organization.

Racial and Ethnic Subcultures

When communicating with individuals of racial and ethnic subcultures, it may require greater effort to understand the diverse cultures that some of these employees come from. Many managers find it difficult to communicate with members of even the most common racial groups in the United States. As our nation becomes ever more culturally diverse, the job of communication becomes even more challenging.

The number of national cultures represented in the United States is very large. As described in Chapter 5, immigration has continued to change the face of America at an ever-increasing rate. Depending on the amount of time an immigrant has been in the United States, one's native culture can produce powerful filters and formidable barriers to aligning subcultural values with organizational values.

We offer several suggestions for communicating with racial subcultures. When we refer to racial subcultures, we are assuming that members of these groups were born and raised in the United States.[19] The first suggestion is to remember that these racial subcultures share the same national culture. Although there is a lot of talk about cultural differences among various racial groups in the United States, we have found, based on our research, that differences tend to be more regional than racial.[20] When setting out to communicate vision and values, it is important to keep in mind that racial subcultures are more alike than different. Generally, racial subcultures share the values of the dominant U.S. culture. Trying to focus too much on cultural differences may inhibit rather than improve communication with members of racial groups.

Second, it is best to ask racial groups how they prefer to be addressed. If you are unsure, it is usually safe to address racial groups as African American, Asian American, Hispanic American, and so forth, acknowledging their ethnic origin and the fact that they are all American by birth and culture.

Lastly, don't use slang that you think the particular racial group uses. In discussing the use of jargon above, we indicated that it was acceptable in certain situations. However, the use of slang with a racial group usually seems contrived and can be interpreted as condescending rather than identifying with members of the group. Since you are communicating with your fellow citizens, you don't have to adjust your communication style, because they should all have approximately the same filters. Sometimes a communicator adjusts his or her communication style because he or she believes that there are significant differences between domestic racial groups. This is not necessary.

The more challenging task is adjusting your communication style to bridge different cultural (ethnic) subcultures. In this case, we are assuming that the individuals in ethnic subcultures are first-generation immigrants that still identify strongly with their native culture. Some helpful strategies for communicating across cultures have been suggested in the communications literature.[21] These include the following:

- *Maintain formality:* Most other cultures value and respect a more formal approach to business dealings. Call others by their titles and family names unless asked to do otherwise. Make sure verbal and nonverbal clues convey propriety and decorum.
- *Show respect:* Listen carefully to what is being communicated and try to understand the other person's feelings. Learn about the other group's culture—its geography, form of government, culture, values, current events, language, and so on.

- *Communicate clearly:* To ensure your oral and written messages are understood, follow these guidelines:

  1. Avoid slang, jargon, and other figures of speech. Expressions such as "they'll eat that up" or "out in left field" are likely to confuse.
  2. Be specific and illustrate your points with concrete examples.
  3. Provide and solicit feedback; summarize frequently; provide a written summary of points presented in the meeting; ask members of the subculture to paraphrase what you've said; encourage questions.
  4. Use a variety of media such as handouts, audiovisual aids, and models.
  5. Avoid attempts at humor; humor doesn't usually translate well.
  6. Speak plainly and slowly, but not too slowly as to appear condescending, and choose your words carefully.

These strategies mirror some of the points that were touched upon earlier. Below are some additional modifications that may need to be considered when communicating with cultural or ethnic subcultures.

1. When using metaphors, analogies, and stories, make sure the cultural subculture is familiar with the context or relationships being described. If in doubt, don't use them until you've had a chance to research appropriate examples from the cultures represented.
2. Social distance varies among cultures. When engaged in face-to-face communication, some cultures desire to be in closer proximity than we may feel comfortable with in the United States. Keep this in mind, and try to adjust when possible.
3. Keep in mind that words in one language may translate differently in another. A commonly cited example is the name Chevrolet selected for one of its models: Nova in Spanish means "no go."
4. Be careful when using body language such as gestures, eye contact, and various postures. Some signs, such as "OK" in the United States, can be an obscenity in another country.

Americans and Canadians value direct eye contact; in many Asian and Latin American countries, however, it is considered to be inappropriate.

Try to keep these precautions in mind when communicating with various cultural and ethnic subcultures to ensure that what you intend to communicate gets beyond cultural filters and is understood in the way you desire.

Gender Subcultures

The popular book *Men Are from Mars, Women Are from Venus* explains in depth how the two sexes communicate in different ways, and several research studies confirm that there are distinctly different communication patterns between males and females.[22] Some of these patterns include the following:

- Women communicate largely to build rapport; men communicate primarily to preserve independence and status by displaying knowledge and skill.
- Men prefer to work out their problems by themselves, whereas women prefer to talk out solutions with another person.
- Women are more likely to compliment the work of a coworker; men are more likely to be critical.
- Men tend to interrupt to dominate a conversation or to change the subject; women tend to interrupt to agree with or support what another person is saying.
- Men tend to be more directive in their conversation, whereas women emphasize politeness.
- Men are more interested than women in calling attention to their own accomplishments.
- Men tend to dominate discussions during meetings.
- Men tend to internalize success ("That's one of my strengths") and to externalize failures ("We should have been given more time"). Women tend to externalize success ("I was lucky") and to internalize failures ("I'm just not good at that").

- In the workplace, men speak differently to other men than they do to women, and women speak differently to other women than they do to men.
- Even when gender is not readily apparent in on-line communication, men and women have recognizably different styles in posting to the Internet.

Recognizing these differences will facilitate communication of vision and values when speaking to groups of men and women. Leaders of organizations should keep these patterns in mind when the opposite gender replies differently or interacts differently than expected. The differences listed above would certainly impact the use of metaphors, analogies, and stories, as well as face-to-face communication.

Some additional recommendations for facilitating communication between genders include the following:

- Use formal title and last name when referring to a person, regardless of gender. Women are often identified by name but without formal titles or acknowledging degree attainment.
- Use neutral job titles that do not imply gender, such as chair instead of chairman.
- Avoid phrases that unnecessarily imply gender, such as "the best woman for the job." Use "the best person for the job" instead.
- Avoid demeaning or stereotypical terms, such as "My girl will handle this"; instead say, "My assistant will handle this."
- Use parallel language, such as Dr. Joe Jones, a dentist, and Dr. Mary Jones, a university professor, instead of Dr. Joe Jones, a dentist, and Mrs. Jones, a beautiful blonde.[23]

Knowledge of these differences should help leaders reach both genders more effectively as they go about the task of communicating vision and values.

Generational Subcultures

The generation gap has been used for eons to explain why parents don't understand their children as they move into adolescence. Today we are finding that generational differences among employees explain differing approaches to work ethic, values, and desire for specific reward structures, among other things, within most organizations. Managers of the "Baby Boom" generation are having a difficult time motivating their Generation Xer and Generation Nexter employees. Growing up with digital technology and constant bombardment by the media has shaped these newer generations in unique ways.

How do communication patterns differ among these generational subcultures? The primary difference is the mode of communication they prefer to use. Generation Nexters have even more experience than Generation Xers with computers. Their preferred mode of communication is the Internet or some other related form of technology, such as instant messaging. They also tend to ignore advertising and traditional advertising formats. This means that technologically advanced media will more effectively communicate vision and values to this generational subculture.

Trying to shape their values may be quite challenging as well. To reach beyond the generation gap requires researching, talking with, and listening to these generational subcultures and then framing a message that they understand and trust. Certainly, it is important to use examples relevant to their own experience. They may not be familiar with personalities that the Boomers would know and respect and may not hold traditional values, so communicating to younger generational subcultures requires selecting metaphors, analogies, and stories from very recent times.

When trying to penetrate these generational filters, leaders may want to consider guerrilla marketing. This concept was developed for the Generation Nexters because they ignore ads devised by and made for Baby Boomers. This is a communication medium that they understand and thus may be an effective way of transmitting what is important not only to them and their friends but to organizations as well. The premise in guerrilla marketing is that Nexters prefer word-of-mouth endorsements from their friends about products. Advertising companies are creating campaigns that go into malls, or other areas where Nexters hang out, and give them products to try, hoping they will like them and tell their friends to buy them.

Movie companies are learning that a segment of Gen-Xers and Nexters tend to view movies on the first day of release and then call all of their friends on their cell phones and tell them whether or not the movie is worth seeing. This has more influence than all of the high-budget ad blitzes on TV and radio that influence the Boomers. These examples reveal the significant challenges in communicating with generational subcultures. We are still learning about these subcultures and how best to convey organizational vision and values to them.

Chapter Summary and Conclusions

In this chapter we have suggested techniques, garnered from the fields of speech communication and social psychology, to use when communicating organizational vision and values to employees. Effective communication often evokes emotional responses in employees and should be memorable enough to motivate them to adopt the organizational vision and values as their own.

In this chapter we also discussed ways to modify communication to more effectively reach various subcultures. By breaking through the cultural filters each of these groups has, organizational vision and values can be conveyed in meaningful and appropriate ways, and subcultures can be brought into alignment with the predominant corporate culture.

Building Commitment to
Vision and Values

A strong case for the importance of vision and values and how these are prerequisites for aligning organizational subcultures was made in Chapters 8 and 9. Information on communicating vision and values was presented in Chapter 10. The creation and communication of vision and values is largely a design issue. The process of building commitment to vision and values is an implementation issue. Unfortunately, in practice, making vision and values work is 5 percent design and 95 percent implementation.

Getting organization-wide commitment to vision and values is a long-term proposition because it involves organizations initiating change at a very basic, yet profound level. This is not just any change, but change that takes place between the ears and in the chest of each and every member of the organization. Gaining organization-wide commitment to vision and values is about winning hearts and minds, but once this change is accomplished, the sky is the limit where organizational performance is concerned.

The central role that vision and values now plays in organizations has developed as the business environment and the social contract between organizations and employees has changed. The old contract was based on the idea that work was rewarded, and as people stayed with the organization, they could expect their pay and benefits to reflect their loyal service over time. The turbulent '90s caused a fundamental shift in this contract, where, to be successful, both employees and leadership needed to commit themselves to the organization's vision. The new contract is based on the idea that organizations don't reward work—they reward results. And from the employees' point of view, the individual desires work that is meaningful, provides opportunities for growth, and creates value.[1]

Recall that values influence vision. We really can't develop an inspiring vision about what we should become without understanding who we are and what we hold dear. And as values are a deeply held set of beliefs that often operate at the subconscious level, understanding is often a difficult task. However, it is impossible to change values if we don't even know what they are. Once vision and values have been determined, it is time to begin making them a reality. The first step in that process is to secure organization-wide commitment to them. However, commitment to new vision and values requires change, and it is important to understand what might block the change.

Barriers to Organizational Change

A number of forces within organizations work against the initiation of change. It is important for managers to understand these forces and work to diffuse them so that commitment to vision and values can be successfully achieved. Barriers to change include the comfort and familiarity of the status quo, senior managers who lack the desire and persistence to make change happen, unreasonable expectations, existing organizational structures, passive and apathetic employees, me-first attitude, lack of trust in organizational leadership, competing goals, and a reactionary modus operandi.

The Status Quo

This barrier comes into play when there is a tendency to maintain things the way they currently exist. Everyone in the organization knows the status quo, and it is usually perceived as comfortable and nonthreatening.

Change is viewed as just the opposite because it requires employees to move beyond both their comfort zones and away from those things they know well. Change is concerned with embracing new ways of thinking and new ways of acting. To many, these changes are viewed as painful at best and harmful at worst. Why would someone want to inflict pain upon themselves or change the rules for success that they know so well? Leaders must provide answers to these questions before they are even asked, or change initiatives will never get off the ground. Employee commitment is greater when the change is attractive to them. When situations are win/win, they tend to be embraced more readily than when some win while others lose.

The status quo also refers to the existing set of core values in an organization. Unless and until organizations develop a set of core values that embraces the need to change and adapt to changing environments, they are destined to be marginal players in an increasingly turbulent and global economy.

Passive Leadership

A lack of desire and persistence on the part of organizational leadership will result in failed efforts. Failed efforts, in turn, make it much harder to initiate change in the future, because those opposed to change within the organization believe they can wear the leadership down or wait the leadership out and in the end get what they want—the status quo. Leaders must be bold and create enthusiasm for change to take root and flourish. They need to send the message that the status quo is not an option, and those resisting, or sabotaging, change efforts will experience negative consequences.

Unreasonable Expectations

When employees do not believe that expectations are realistic, it is unreasonable to expect them to give their all to make change happen. Commitment to vision and values is based on the idea that if you can dream it, you can be it. But in all fairness, employees usually have a pretty good idea about what is achievable and what is not. Sometimes it is necessary to outline the path to the end result. For example, when a strategic vision is broken down into its incremental steps, employees can see how achieving one thing acts as a stepping-stone to achieving the next thing. Although the jump from point A to point Z may seem unrealistic, the movement from one point to the next may be realistically achievable.

Change Resistant Structures

Organizational structures that are highly bureaucratic and/or autocratic naturally resist change. Bureaucracy is a structure that relies on several layers of management to get things done. This structure is neither flexible nor adaptable. Autocratic organizations are characterized by leadership that tells people what to do and does not seek their input into how things should be done. Autocratic organizations are usually made up of people that have very low levels of commitment or buy-in concerning the long-term future of the organization. Both conditions lead to an overly controlled environment in which passion for the work is driven out. It is almost impossible to get people to be committed to great things without passion.

Apathetic Employees

The existence of apathetic employees may be the result of bureaucratic structures and/or autocratic leadership, or they may result from some other form of leadership dereliction. Leaders want motivated and engaged workers. In a recent survey of chief executives from a broad cross-section of companies, CEOs were very clear that finding enough motivated employees was one of their biggest challenges—and frustrations.[2] This survey suggested that part of the problem stares back at them every day in the mirror. Leaders need to outline a clear and convincing strategic vision—something that employees want to make happen because it contributes to a greater cause. This vision is based in a set of core values that makes unambiguous what the organization is all about and helps guide decision making throughout the firm.

When people know what is valued and where leaders are trying to take the organization, the chance of finding motivated employees is greatly increased. Another thing that leads to passive and apathetic employees is when they perceive their work to be boring or meaningless. When work becomes mundane and employees fail to see how their efforts contribute to something great, they are likely to have little passion and, subsequently, little commitment to helping the organization realize its potential.

Me-First Attitude

When people put their personal needs (at work) ahead of the organization's needs, organizational values are not strong. When employees have a "me-first" mind-set, subcultural values flourish, and unity of purpose is very low or even nonexistent.

Lack of Trust in Leadership

A formidable barrier to change is a lack of trust in leadership. As stated in Chapter 8, trust in leadership is crucial when it comes to inspiring others to embrace a vision for the future. Without trust in leaders (and the decisions they make), it is hard to expect change to occur within the organization. Unfortunately, trust can take a long time to develop—years in some cases. But until it does, not much is going to happen.

Competing Goals

Another barrier to change is when the organization has competing (or inconsistent) goals, either within the overall organization or between organizational units. Inconsistency is due to ineffective or incompetent leadership. Research in organizational behavior has shown that well-developed goals can be a powerful and motivating force for achievement and change. However, it is clear that competing goals cannot be achieved. When employees are working against each other, the result is confusion and frustration. Leaders need to make sure that organizational goals are properly aligned and provide consistency across units.

Reactionary Modus Operandi

Finally, when organizations have a reactionary modus operandi, they are constantly responding to events rather than shaping them. Organizations that are continually in a reactionary mode rarely are successful in developing the kind of commitment that is necessary to achieve strategic visions or develop the values upon which they are based. Reactionary organizations are usually focused on short-term performance or current events and not on a long-term vision of what the organization wants to become.

Taken together, these forces can be significant barriers, and one can see that developing commitment to vision and values is not an easy thing to do. Many conditions can derail these efforts. However, leaders who are cognizant of these barriers and take steps to eliminate them before change efforts are initiated are in a stronger position to effect change.

The Role of Leadership

Numerous attempts have been made to find the "magic bullet" of corporate success, and in the end, a significant part of the answer is always found to be effective leadership. This book is no different in that regard. When it comes to developing and nurturing core values and establishing a viable strategic vision, leadership is the alpha and the omega of organizational success. As important as leadership is to establishing vision and values, it is even more important in building commitment to them. So, how are leaders able to persuade employees to commit to organizational vision and values? Part of the answer lies in who they are, what they do, and the skills they possess. Some of the more important factors in this process include the ability to create the perceived need to change, a cross-functional mind-set, sensitivity to the importance of vision and values, a high level of trust in employees, the ability to fulfill their symbolic role, intercultural competence, ongoing in-depth training, development of standards of behavior, ability to gain trust, ability to manage and shape perceptions, high expectations, and charisma.

When you think about the magnitude of the change involved, the task seems daunting indeed. It is often easier for leaders from the outside to initiate major change because they do not carry any organizational baggage associated with the status quo. That aside, vision and values initiatives are usually associated with the person at the top who, by necessity, is able to persuade important groups and individuals in the firm to commit themselves to new directions and then energize them to make it happen. In a large organization these efforts are spread over thousands of employees.

One of the "techniques" that leaders can use to help the effort spread is to *point to a need to change* due to a potential or impending crisis. A crisis helps develop a sense of urgency where foot-dragging is not an option. Getting buy-in to vision and values can take a tremendous investment of time, energy, talent, and money. When people perceive the need to change and that it must be done immediately because of a crisis, they tend to grasp the importance of change, work to find solutions, and then implement them in great haste. When companies are close to the edge, it gets people's attention.

A cross-functional mind-set allows leaders to see the "big picture" of the organization, and this helps them to understand how the different units (including subcultures) must work together to move the organization forward. When leaders have a cross-functional view, they understand the need to develop interpersonal networks and the importance of individuals and groups identifying with the company as a whole.[3] Another way to express this is that leaders need to be "systems thinkers" who can conceptualize the organization as a whole, not just as the sum of its parts. And they must be able to visualize how this whole will evolve in the future. When leaders have these conceptual skills they are better able to develop a comprehensive plan that unifies the different parts of the organization.

Leaders also must be *sensitive to the importance of vision and values to long-term success*. Although many managers are not comfortable with this "soft" side of leadership, they must openly express their understanding and commitment to these ends. They must continually talk about them, write about them, and find ways to reinforce efforts toward achieving them. In this regard they are part coach, part cheerleader, and part salesman.

Leaders trying to develop commitment to vision and values must also demonstrate *a high level of trust in employees*. Effective leaders realize that they do not get things done by themselves. While they may be the "straw that stirs the drink," leaders are not the ingredients for success; these come from getting the right people in the right places within the organization. Effective leaders guard and nurture the vision and values and necessarily delegate many decisions to others. They rely on these decisions to be consistent with the vision and values, and this requires a high degree of trust. Although some may imagine the macho manager sitting at the apex of the organization making all of the critical decisions, in reality (for successful companies, anyway) this is far from the truth. Leaders must passionately own their vision and values and then work with others to move the organization forward. In this way vision and values act as guides to organizational actions and decision making.

Effective leaders *fulfill their role as symbolic managers* and recognize the important role that they play in nurturing the values and creating the vision. As a symbolic manager, no event is too trivial to recognize and participate in. Symbolic managers have hundreds of opportunities each day to influence values and articulate the vision that they have established for the organization. In many cases, they can do both in the same episode. Every day the life of a leader is full of events, some trivial, some noteworthy, and some very important. One of the skills of an effective leader is to distinguish among these and respond appropriately. The way a leader responds to these events establishes credibility and reinforces the culture. To make a big deal out of trivial things makes a leader look foolish. To overlook big things makes a leader look like a villain or victim. To miss an event or one's cues when something noteworthy happens makes a leader look insensitive, uncaring, or stupid. Leaders must understand these distinctions and never miss an opportunity to reinforce the vision and values that they are trying to achieve.[4]

Effective leaders must also possess a certain degree of *intercultural competence.* As stated earlier, the existence of subcultures within an organization often serves to pull it in different directions. Managers with intercultural competence understand the history, religion, art, and often languages of the cultural groups they interact with. This understanding helps them to bridge the gap between cultures and allows them to persuade others that the organization's vision and values must be achieved.

As conditions continue to change, it is important that leaders are *continually seeking in-depth training.* Effective leaders are continually learning by exposing themselves to new ideas, technologies, business practices, and cultures through both in-house and external training, and through reading, discussions, and travel. Although the shelf-life of some knowledge is timeless, for others it is very short, and the only way to stay on top of things (or even be in a position to ask informed questions) is through continual learning.

Leaders must also *develop organization-wide and personal standards of behavior,* and these are not necessarily the same. Hypervalues must be expressed throughout the organization, and a clear, unambiguous vision must be articulated as well. Hypervalues set a non-negotiable standard of conduct for the entire organization, but leaders should set an even higher standard and then look for ways to exhibit these behaviors. Through this process of modeling behaviors the organization will come to see what the core values are and how leaders live them.[5]

For example, Herb Kelleher at Southwest Airlines has generated intense loyalty and commitment to a set of values by the way he models them. He tries to remember employees' names and asks about their personal lives. After asking pilots to freeze their salaries for several years to keep costs down, he did the same. He is notorious for "getting his hands dirty" by rolling up his sleeves and helping baggage handlers, ticket agents, and flight attendants. His humor (he has dressed in a bunny suit and leprechaun outfit and then proceeded to serve snacks and drinks on flights) serves as an example for employees to "join in the fun" of working for Southwest Airlines. Kelleher's philosophy is built on the ideas that he must work harder than anyone else to show what it means to work for Southwest and that he is deeply devoted to the business.

After Kelleher exhibited the core values that he wanted to ingrain in Southwest, employees were eager to get on board. Stories of how employees have gone above and beyond the call of duty at Southwest have become legendary. A Southwest pilot flew a passenger to Houston for transplant surgery after the passenger had missed his connection; a ticket agent watched a passenger's dog for two weeks after the passenger showed up at the gate at the last minute without a proper dog kennel; another ticket agent allowed a passenger who was traveling to Phoenix for medical treatment to stay with her for two weeks. Do you see commitment here?

Southwest workers have also been known to go out of their way to surprise, amuse, or somehow entertain passengers. During delays, ticket agents have been known to award prizes to the passenger with the largest hole in his or her sock; they are encouraged to make entertaining announcements, such as asking passengers to pass plastic cups to the aisle so that they can be washed and used for the next group of passengers; and one flight attendant had the habit of hiding in the overhead luggage bin and popping out when passengers started filing on board.

The *ability to gain trust* is another key ingredient for a successful leader. Why? Because getting commitment to vision and values implies change, and change creates instability. In times of instability people turn to relationships for guidance, and the quality of these relationships is largely based on trust. So how can leaders gain the trust that underlies employees' commitment? The answer is straightforward: people are won over one at a time when leaders are open and fair, express their feelings, tell the truth, show consistency, fulfill their promises, and maintain confidences. However, perhaps the most important thing that leaders can do to develop trust is to be as transparent as possible when it comes to things like letting people know their intentions. Policies, procedures, strategies, tactics, rewards, and recognition must be clear and applied with integrity.

Leaders also *manage and shape perceptions*. Although this may sound Machiavellian, in truth it is all part of developing a following. To the extent that leaders develop the perception that they are smart, personable, decisive, verbally adept, aggressive, committed to the organization, caring, empathetic, hard-working, and consistent in their words and actions, they increase the chances that they will be viewed as an effective leader. People are more likely to commit themselves to leaders whom they view in a favorable light.

It is also important that leaders have *high expectations for their companies and employees*. When leaders expect great things from their employees, they often go to great lengths to prove the leader right. When leaders do not think that employees are capable of significant achievement, workers seldom disappoint. The expectations of leaders influence how they interact with their subordinates. Part of creating vision and values lies in the belief that organizations can do great things. When leaders truly believe this, and they expect the organization to embrace these ideals, people are often willing to commit themselves to the task.

Another characteristic of effective leaders is charisma. "Old-school" thinking held that either you were born with charisma or you weren't. The fact is that charisma can be learned, at least the parts of it that are needed to secure buy-in to vision and values. Charismatic behaviors include things like the ability to project a powerful, confident, and dynamic presence, the ability to articulate vision and values that inspire people to make them happen, and the ability to communicate high expectations and the confidence in others' ability to meet these expectations.[6] Although charisma without substance will lead nowhere, when the two come together, employees will quickly recognize this and respond accordingly.

Leaders also must understand that the process of achieving vision and values does not happen overnight. The way companies attain them is by continually making progress in the right direction. This requires leaders to have the fortitude and persistence to make fundamental change happen.

Gaining Commitment and Making It Stick

As stated previously, vision and values must resonate with employees by going beyond lofty sentiments and touching the people's hearts and minds. When employees understand that they belong to a great organization that is committed to doing truly meaningful things, they are more likely to bring passion with them to their jobs. With passion people can do amazing things. All employees, but especially those in management positions, must understand how local or subculture change initiatives are connected to broader organizational efforts so they can be partners in the change process and thereby help persuade others to come along.

In change efforts it is necessary to start with the "who" and not with the "what." The first challenge for leaders is to get the right people (i.e., employees who are motivated to ensure the organization's success) in the right places within the organization. Not until the right people are recruited will positive things begin to happen. An added benefit is that others often decide to come along because of who is already on the team. Once the right people are in place, the problem of trying to motivate them largely goes away because they tend to motivate themselves. To the right people, the promise of the achievement of great things produces an inner drive that is more powerful than any motivational technique. Great vision and values without great people will not achieve great results.

In addition, it is unrealistic to expect the organizational subcultures to commit to vision and values if it is not clear that organizational leadership has done so. Once the right people are in place they must be united in purpose, and that purpose is driven by their own commitment to the organization's direction. Despite the excitement that vision and values often inspire, the process of building shared vision across the organization is often mundane. Managers need to weave discussions of vision and values into the daily life of the organization. Rarely is a substantial shift marked by an event or a point in time; it happens incrementally over a long period of time. Progress toward achieving vision and values is made as leaders make decisions and solve problems with vision and values in mind. As more and more people throughout the organization do the same, progress accelerates.

The climate is ripe for leaders to infuse vision and values initiatives in their organizations. So how can leaders help infuse an organization with vision and values? The answers lie in a consistent set of actions that inspire passion, promote unity, and reinforce those things that are considered central and foundational to the organization. It is worth noting that commitment comes about because of a deeply held belief. In this regard, commitment to vision is almost identical to commitment to any core value. As such, we believe that the path to individual commitment to both vision and values is very similar. Figure 11.1 shows how some of the elements mentioned in Chapter 9 interact to develop and sustain commitment to vision and values. Artifacts, behaviors, and espoused values can all reinforce and support core beliefs and ideals. It should be noted that all of the elements impact behaviors and vision and core values. In terms of artifacts, status symbols, power structures, routines, facilities layout, language, stories, heroes and villains, systems and processes, and rewards and recognition all must be coordinated to develop and sustain commitment to vision and values.

Make Use of Status Symbols

Status symbols consist of physical things that are highly valued within an organization. When critics blasted Napoleon for reinstating the largely symbolic Legion of Honor medal, he replied, "You lead men by baubles, not words." Although this view may be more than a little naïve, it does illustrate a point about human nature: small gestures can be very meaningful.[7] Examples of status symbols might include a large office, close-in

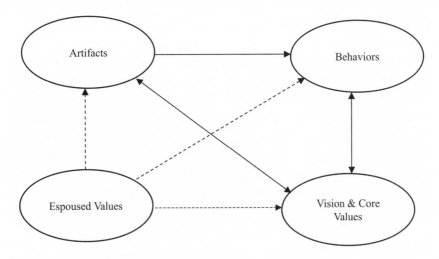

FIGURE 11.1   Reinforcing and Sustaining Vision and Values

parking, a symbol of achievement such as a lapel pin or a different-colored hard hat. The point is that those who exhibit exemplary behaviors that support the vision and values should earn status symbols.

Make Use of Power Structures

Power structures influence the way the organization really works. Power can come from position, seniority, information, personality, achievement, or any number of other factors. Power structures are directly related to the ability to influence opinion in an organization and to make change happen.

Make Use of Routines

Routine refers to the way something is done on a regular basis. Routines can be either formal or informal, but they should reflect the firm's vision and values. Vision and values have been supported in some companies with corporate songs, cheers, affirmations, or pledges that reinforce psychological commitment.[8]

Make Use of Facilities Layout

The physical attributes of a workplace, or facilities layout, determine work flow and influence relationships. Other aspects of layout include look and feel, privacy, common space, sense of place, cleanliness, organization, signage, recognition areas, and event promotion, to name a few. An organization that is proud of itself will reflect this through its physical environment. Consistency from one department to another and, for organizations with multiple locations, from one site to another, is important. Lavish headquarters and spartan field facilities send a negative message to the organization that there is an "us" versus "them" mentality.

Make Use of Language

Language concerns more than just dialect. It has to do with tone, civility, expressions, use of slang or professional jargon, and so on. As the foundation of all communication, language should never be used to manipulate or make others feel inferior. Language is a concern when it comes to uniting subcultures; when people don't speak the same language because of membership in a subculture, the big picture tends to get lost, and there is a tendency to revert to subcultural norms. Language can also be used to reinforce a frame of reference and a sense of belonging to a special group through the use of terminology such as "cast members," "associates," or "Motorolans."[9]

Make Use of Stories

Stories provide a rich source of information, especially for new hires. Stories often illustrate how someone inside the organization handled a situation in an exemplary manner, and thus they serve as concrete examples of desirable behaviors and the organization's core values. For example, during new employee orientation at Nordstrom, employees are not lectured on how to deliver superior customer service out of a company manual. Rather, they are told stories of instances where employees have gone out of their way to provide superior customer service—such as when an employee accepted a return on a purchase that was over two years old with no questions asked. By illustrating values with behaviors, new employees are made to see how superior service has been delivered and how high the bar has been set.

Make Use of Heroes and Villains

From an organizational point of view, the identification of heroes and villains ensures that a clear distinction is drawn between the "good guys" and the "bad guys." Good guys are those who can help the organization realize visions and values and bad guys are those who stand in the way. Heroes can come from inside or outside the organization, but villains are usually outsiders. Heroes are celebrated for their abilities to think beyond existing boundaries and to find extraordinary ways to contribute to the vision and values. People within organizations look up to heroes and try to emulate them. In railroad parlance, management makes the trains run on time; heroes get the engine going.

As noted previously, leaders communicate vision and values in daily conversations and in organizational ceremonies and rituals. Employees that exhibit the values in exemplary ways are recognized and given the status of organizational "values heroes." Older employees mentor younger workers, and through the mentoring process, the values are transferred. Heroes are important because they show that success is attainable, provide role models, symbolize the organization to the outside world, embody what makes the organization special, set a standard of performance, and motivate employees to be like them.[10] All of these promote high levels of commitment.

Make Use of Systems and Processes

Systems and processes define organizational activities, and they must be consistent with one another and the organization's vision and values. Once a decision has been made about vision and values, the challenge becomes how to make sure that everyone in the company internalizes them. To be meaningful, vision and values need to be integrated into all important organizational processes and decisions. For example, they should guide the process by which an organization recruits potential employees. Position advertising should reflect the vision and values to attract those who are predisposed to embrace them.

People should be recruited because of their ability to fit the organization, not just the job. In addition, interview questions should probe the experience of candidates as it relates to supporting the organization's vision and values. Efforts should be made to find out what excites potential hires and what inspires them to do their best. Job-specific scenarios can be developed that conclude with a dilemma in which the candidate must make a decision and then explain how and why the decision was made. Candidates who exhibit a tendency toward the organization's vision and values should more readily commit to them.

In addition to the intake process, orientation and subsequent training should be based on the vision and values to create the expectation that they will be followed. Further, employee performance evaluations should be tied to behaviors that reinforce the vision and values; then performance feedback should be given with emphasis on how employees are contributing to the vision and values and on areas that need work. Finally, in termination cases, it should be made clear why termination was necessary. Tying unacceptable behavior to vision and values usually makes a strong case, especially if an employee has been promoted throughout his or her tenure with the organization.

An organization also needs to be relentless in promoting the vision and values on a day-to-day basis. Employees need to be aware of the inherent connection between the organization's values and the decisions they make every day in dealing with outside parties such as vendors and customers. Employees will not accept and embrace vision and values unless they are continually communicated and promoted. For example, Ritz-Carlton Hotels has adopted a core value based on superior customer service, and all employees at every property are expected to embrace this value and find ways to make it happen. To reinforce it, at the beginning of each shift, employees from each work group (front desk, maintenance, housekeeping, restaurants) discuss how they will deliver superior customer service and share recent examples of it in their unit. Over time, employees don't have to recite the values to keep them front and center in their minds because they have internalized them by living the behaviors that make it a reality.

Make Use of Rewards and Recognition

Rewards and recognition are crucial to getting organizational commitment to vision and values. There is an old saying that goes, "You don't get what you want, you get what you reward." Rewarding behaviors encourages people to repeat those behaviors. And the more behaviors are repeated, the more subconscious (core) they become. Rewards and recognition are best delivered through rites and rituals. Through participation in these organizational ceremonies, people can loosen up and have a little fun—and feel that they belong to a special community. The importance of this process cannot be overemphasized; through these rituals people learn what is important and thus come to understand the organization's behavioral norms. Every event is an opportunity to reinforce vision and values: people who exhibit or support the core values receive rewards, and those who do not support them do not receive rewards.

Recognition works in a similar manner as reward but with two distinct advantages: it is less expensive, and it is usually more effective. Managers who take the time to personally congratulate someone for something done well or write a note acknowledging an employee's accomplishments can count on a positive response and a repeat of the desired behavior. For people who desire social acceptance, public recognition often encourages future desirable behaviors. Groups can also be acknowledged for their contributions in meetings or company gatherings.[11] All of these mechanisms serve to perpetuate the vision and values and help ensure that they become part of the subconscious foundation of the organization.[12]

Another important element shown in Figure 11.1 is behaviors. Behaviors both affect vision and values and are affected by them. In fact, the two go hand in hand. When people throughout the organization have embraced vision and values, they act at the subconscious level to guide actions and decision making. And as explained above, the more times that a desirable behavior is repeated, the more ingrained that behavior becomes. When behaviors become so ingrained that they are simply part of the way things are done, like at Ritz-Carlton, the underlying vision and values are constantly reinforced.

It is important for organizations to communicate how they want their employees to behave and to establish the boundaries of acceptable decorum.

Another way that vision and values can be promoted is through ongoing communication that reminds employees of what the values are. Communicating values is limited only by managerial creativity, but examples include the distribution of values reminders such as embossed "values cards" or coffee mugs with the values listed on them—anything to keep reminding employees of the core value set. Further, the values can be reinforced by having them briefly discussed at the beginning of company, department, or committee meetings.

Finally, examples of behaviors that model commitment to vision and values can be distributed with very little cost via e-mail. These messages should illustrate how a value was exhibited in some way either within a unit, a division, or the whole organization. It is not terribly important that employees be able to regurgitate vision and values on command; rather, vision and values should be internalized by everyone in the organization and result in behaviors that help achieve them. The impact of vision and values is greatest when they operate at the subconscious level. Employees don't have to reflect on them to make decisions; they make decisions quickly and easily because it is the "right" thing to do. It is right because it is consistent with the organization's values, and it is quick and easy because they have been thoroughly internalized—the vision and values are a part of who they are.

The third element that shapes vision and values is espoused values. Espoused values are a starting point; they are the ideals that the company wants to achieve. Espoused values might address areas such as the company's desired image or its business philosophies. To the extent that espoused values are genuine and the organization commits to them, they will positively affect behaviors as well as vision and core values. In addition, if an organization is serious about them, artifacts should then be aligned to reinforce them. However, the broken lines in Figure 11.1 underscore the point that espoused values are not necessarily ingrained and, as such, are weaker than core beliefs.

Chapter Summary and Conclusions

A major point made in this chapter is that it is important for managers to understand the various barriers to strategic change and work to diffuse them so that commitment to vision and values can be obtained. Another major point is that when it comes to developing and nurturing core values and establishing a viable strategic vision, leadership is the alpha and the omega of organizational success. Finally, in terms of gaining commitment to values and vision and making this commitment stick, artifacts, behaviors, and espoused values can all reinforce and support core values and vision.

One of the wonderful things about vision and values is that once a company has them, they tend to perpetuate themselves over and over again. As commitment to vision and values grows and positive change begins to happen, success breeds success. In fact, it is important for leaders to look for and exploit some sustainable successes early on.[13] We can return to the metaphor of the flywheel—it takes a lot of effort to get the flywheel to spin, but once it does, its own momentum allows subsequent turns to be accomplished in less time and with less effort. Getting commitment to vision and values can be hard work, can cost a fortune, and take what seems like forever. Leaders must be convinced that the changes are necessary and the need is real. However, in the end, great things won't happen unless and until commitment to vision and values is obtained.

There are very few hallelujah breakthroughs when it comes to getting commitment to vision and values. When change happens over time, it may appear very dramatic from the outside, but that is usually not how it feels on the inside. There is no such thing as a one-step transformation. Transformation happens over long periods as organizations evolve, and this evolution takes place one day at a time. However, be assured that with organizational commitment to a clear vision and strong core values, positive transformation will happen.

Maintaining Subculture Alignment

Once all of the steps in the strategic change approach have been taken, the ideal situation is that all organizational subcultures have been properly aligned with the predominant corporate culture. Assuming that all steps in the process have been properly executed, and the subcultures are indeed aligned, the task now becomes maintaining this alignment. In the next few sections of this chapter we focus on some things that executive leadership and change agents can do to facilitate the accomplishment of this task.

Incorporate Change into Your Corporate Culture

The task of maintaining subculture alignment is much simpler if change is part of corporate culture. In other words, executive leadership should communicate that change is an expected and permanent part of the organization's culture. The type of change we refer to here is not strategic change but incremental change that is continuous. In other words, counter to conventional wisdom, leaders may have to initiate change simply to impress upon employees that change is expected. However, change for change's sake should be an exercise that yields some type of positive result. That is, the focus of incremental change should result in continuous improvement to organizational processes, tasks, operations, and so on.

The issue that executive leadership must resolve is how to persuade employees that there is a need for continuous change. One strategy is to administer surveys periodically to tap into employee opinions and concerns. For example, executive leadership might periodically survey employees for their opinions about processes that might need to be improved, problems that need to be solved, or issues that need to be resolved. Providing employees with survey feedback from these periodic surveys does a couple of things. First, it allows employees to take the lead in continuous change efforts. Moreover, the multitude of problems and issues identified by employees ensures that there are enough things to be done to justify continuous change.

Second, allowing employees to lead continuous change efforts reduces their natural resistance to change. Also, the fact that they have identified the problems that need to be solved, the issues that need to be resolved, or processes that need improving negates perceptions that executive leadership is simply ordering unnecessary change. These two strategies do not require much effort, but their implementation makes employees more receptive to continuous change. If the goal is to maintain subculture alignment, organizations have to cement continuous change into their culture—into the way things are done in the organization.[1]

Provide Effective Change Leadership

Once continuous change becomes a part of an organization's corporate culture, a mechanism is in place that not only renders employees receptive to change but also facilitates the monitoring of factors that lead to subculture misalignment. However, executive leadership must reinforce these continuous change efforts and employees' commitment to them by providing effective change leadership. Behaviors associated with effective change leadership have been identified in the literature. Leaders are encouraged to do the following:

- Develop and tell employees stories regarding their personal history, values, and strategic vision for the organization.
- Develop and tell employees stories regarding the organization's history, values, and strategic vision.
- Demonstrate to employees the connections between their individual goals and the organization's strategic vision.

- Choose three important values and determine how to live them out in front of employees.
- In each encounter, treat each employee as if he or she mattered.
- Circulate among employees.
- Celebrate employees' accomplishments.
- Embrace and value diversity (for example, cultural, gender, functional diversity among employees).
- Listen to the voices of employees.
- Ask employees for suggestions and implement them as appropriate.
- Provide employees with honest, ongoing feedback.
- Explain their intentions and actions.[2]

Strengthen the Cultural Network

As suggested in the introduction to this book, cultural homogeneity (that is, members of subcultures subscribe to a set of core organizational values and the strategic vision) is maintained through a cultural network. This network is an aspect of social information processing.[3] The notion behind social information processing is that individuals, as adaptive organisms, adapt attitudes, behaviors, and beliefs to their social context and to the reality of their own past and present behavior and situation. The organization's cultural network, then, is designed to convey the values of the corporate culture to organization members.

The network produces cultural homogeneity (shared values and vision) throughout the organization, which, in turn, helps to create and maintain a strong corporate culture. Essentially, the cultural network is a communication network that connects employees within the organization. Thus, subculture alignment can be maintained in the organization by using the cultural network to distribute the type of information that is designed to build commitment to vision and values. However, leaders must be sure that they understand the different nuances of the cultural network as well as the advantages and disadvantages of using it for this purpose. The pitfall to avoid is the entanglement of the cultural network with the organization's grapevine.

If organizational subcultures are rarely in precise alignment with the predominant corporate culture, then the cultural network is failing to produce cultural homogeneity throughout the entire organization. In other words, shared values and vision are not being transmitted to organizational members as effectively as they could (or should) be. If the cultural diagnosis indicates that the organizational subcultures are misaligned, chances are the organization's cultural network is not operating properly. Either the wrong type of information is being transmitted through it, the information is being transmitted in an untimely fashion, or the cultural network has experienced an information overload, has been short-circuited, or has experienced failure.

Whatever the reason, the cultural network should be evaluated to determine its effectiveness. If the network defies evaluation, because of the cost involved, the difficulty of evaluation, or the intangible nature of some cultural networks, there are methods that can be used to increase the probability that members of all organizational subcultures will be exposed to and agree on organizational values and vision. A relatively simple method is to examine the content of the organization's annual reports, newsletters, press releases, and magazines.[4] What does the organization say about itself to its employees?

Organizations that desire to maintain an alignment among organizational subcultures make statements about their values and beliefs to the extent that they become ingrained and so powerful that they affect their employees' day-to-day behavior on, and even off, the job. As a control measure, policies (or strong encouragement) that require employees to read organizational publications on a regular basis might be instituted. Also, re-surveying employees using a random sampling technique over the course of several months can be used to monitor whether the alignment is being maintained. This can help determine the effectiveness of the strategic change.

Hone and Apply Various Skills

Managing the strategic change process and maintaining the results of the change requires an unusually broad and finely honed set of leadership skills. Chief among these are political, systems, and people skills.

- *Political skills.* Organizations play host to hot and intensely political games, and the lower the stakes of the game, the more intense the politics. As change agents, leaders should not be players, but they need to understand the game. This is one area where leaders must make their own judgments and keep their own counsel; no one can do it for them. However, knowing the game will provide leaders with some insights into what must be done to maintain subculture alignment.

• *Systems skills.* A system is an arrangement of resources and routines intended to produce specified results. Thus, systems reflect organizations, and by the same token, organizations can be considered systems. There are "hard systems" (for example, manufacturing, computer, and so on) within organizations as well as "soft" systems (for example, compensation systems, appraisal systems, promotion systems, and reward and incentive systems).

As change agents, leaders will find that systems skills are very important to have. For example, leaders must be able to take apart and reassemble these "hard" and "soft" systems in novel ways and then determine the political impacts of what they have learned about them. Analysis of these systems and projections of their potential political and other impacts will also provide leaders with insights into what must be done to maintain subculture alignment.

• *People skills.* Employees are the sine qua non of organizations, and they come in all manner of sizes, shapes, colors, intelligence and ability levels, gender, sexual preferences, national origins, first and second languages, religious beliefs, attitudes toward life and work, personalities, and priorities—and these are just a few of the dimensions along which employees vary. As change agents, leaders will have to deal with them all. The skills most needed in this area are those that typically fall under the heading of communication or interpersonal skills. To be effective, leaders must be able to listen and listen actively, to restate, to reflect, to clarify without interrogating, to lead or channel a discussion, to plant ideas, and to develop them. Moreover, leaders will have to learn to speak Systems, Marketing, Manufacturing, Finance, Personnel, Legal, and a host of other organizational dialects. Again, honing this skill will provide valuable insights into what leaders need to do to maintain subculture alignment.[5]

Build Integrity into the Process

As change agents, the most important personal tool leaders can use to align organizational subcultures and maintain this alignment is integrity. Employees' positive perception of a leader's integrity binds them to the organization's strategic vision and the core set of organizational values. When leaders act consistently with organizational vision and values, employees take notice, and leadership integrity further expands.[6] Living with integrity means avoiding deceptive communication, either overtly or by omission, and being honest. Moreover, living with rigorous honesty gives employees confidence that every step in the strategic change process is ethically sound.

There are several ethical issues that should be considered during the strategic change approach to aligning organizational subcultures. Ensuring that these ethical issues are resolved not only facilitates subculture alignment but helps to maintain the alignment. A sample of issues raised during the strategic change process include the misuse of data, the ownership of data, coercion, and confidentiality.[7]

- *Misuse of data.* An ethical breach occurs when data collected from surveys are distorted, deleted, or not reported by the change agent, or when the data are used to assess groups (for example, subcultures) punitively, resulting in personal, professional, or organizational harm. Deletion or distortion of data may also result in a misleading diagnosis, thereby making subsequent steps in the process invalid.
- *Ownership of data.* An ethical dilemma is raised when feedback from survey data is not shared with all contributing participants. Important questions, such as, "How do we roll out the survey data, who receives it first, how is it delivered?" must be addressed. Too often these questions are left unanswered until the survey data come back and are ready for distribution. Sometimes the data are negative, surprising the senior levels of the organization. How confidential is this information? What if customers see it? What if top corporate leaders see it? There are often ethical dilemmas surrounding a lack of candor, openness, and truth.

- *Coercion.* When employees are forced to participate in a change effort (for example, completing surveys), an ethical issue is raised. The basic issue concerns "free will," in the sense that executive leaders "force" employees to abridge their personal values or needs against their will. If employees are coerced into participating, the validity of the data is called into question.
- *Confidentiality.* Because electronic mail is rapidly becoming such a large part of organizations' communications systems, there are ethical issues that should be considered when e-mail surveys are administered to employees. For example, an electronic response is never truly anonymous, since the individual(s) collecting the survey data see the respondents' e-mail addresses. As suggested in Chapter 7, these individuals are ethically required to guard the confidentiality of the respondents and to assure respondents that they will do so.

Maintaining subculture alignment requires much work and attention. However, by incorporating change into corporate culture, providing effective change leadership, strengthening the organization's cultural network, and building integrity into the strategic change process, leaders can guide their organizations to superior performance.

A Final Review

We end this final chapter by briefly reviewing the steps in the strategic change approach to aligning organizational subcultures. As the modified model in Figure 12.1 indicates, step 1 begins with diagnosing the corporate culture. Actions taken during this step include collecting information, using one of three approaches: surveys, interviews, or observations. If information collected from these approaches reveals that organizational subcultures are in alignment (that is, corporate culture is strong), the model indicates that organizational performance should be monitored. This task might be viewed as an extra step (step 6) in the process. Implied at this step is that in addition to monitoring performance, periodic diagnoses of corporate culture should be conducted to check for misalignments.

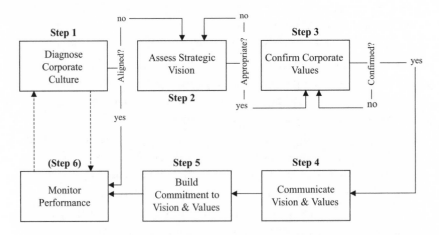

FIGURE 12.1   Modified Model of the Strategic Change Approach

If information collected from the diagnosis step reveals that organizational subcultures are not in alignment (that is, corporate culture is weak), corollary actions include sharing data that show dysfunctional effects of subculture misalignments and providing plausible explanations and evidence to organization members showing why a corporate culture change is needed. Also if misalignment is revealed in step 1, step 2 of the strategic change approach is to assess the strategic vision of the organization. Since this approach is vision driven, it is imperative that top managers of organizations have a clearly articulated strategic vision and assess whether it is appropriate for the organization. If it is not, the assessment process should be repeated until there is consensus among all organizational participants concerning its appropriateness. (We acknowledge here that consensus among all organizational participants may be wishful thinking. However, the astute manager will have a feel for when enough and the "right" participants have bought into the vision process.)

Once "consensus" is reached concerning the appropriateness of the strategic vision, step 3 in the strategic change approach is to confirm corporate values. It is imperative that organizations confirm their values by clearly establishing what they are, promoting them, and practicing them. If the values cannot be confirmed, this step should be repeated until they are. Of course, if the survey conducted in step 1 indicates that the subcultures share similar values, step 3 can be skipped. However, if the survey indicates that the subcultures do not share similar values, efforts to promote and practice these values should be increased. After a reasonable period of time has passed (3–6 months), another survey should be conducted. Keep repeating this step until the results confirm that values are aligned. A word of caution: repeating the same survey over and over may give you false results, especially once employees catch on to what you are trying to accomplish.

Once organizational values have been confirmed, step 4 in the strategic change approach is to communicate the strategic vision and corporate values, using techniques such as framing, simple language, multiple forums, repetition, and tailoring them to each organizational subculture. Once vision and values have been communicated, step 5 of the strategic change approach is to build commitment to the strategic vision and corporate values. This entails, among other things, creating a sense in employees that they belong to an organization that is special.

By way of closing remarks, we acknowledge that using the strategic change approach to aligning organizational subcultures can be a significant undertaking for many organizations, especially if resources are scarce. However, considering the alternative (losing competitive advantage), finding the financial and time resources to implement this approach is probably worth the effort. In this book we have provided a relatively inexpensive cost-effective approach to assessing subculture misalignments, realigning subcultures, and maintaining their alignment. We are confident that this approach will help organizations gain the competitive advantage they seek.

Notes

Chapter 1: Introduction

1. M. E. Porter, *Competitive Strategy: Techniques for Analyzing Industries and Competitors* (New York: Free Press, 1980).

2. The sample of companies using these generic strategies was taken from C. W. L. Hill and G. R. Jones, *Strategic Management: An Integrated Approach* (Boston: Houghton Mifflin, 2001); and J. A. Pearce III and R. B. Robinson Jr., *Strategic Management: Formulation, Implementation, and Control* (Boston: McGraw-Hill, 2003).

3. For a fuller discussion of the distinctive competence concept, see C. K. Prahalad and G. Hamel, "The core competence of the corporation," *Harvard Business Review* 68 (1990): 79–93.

4. R. S. Teitelbaum, "Keeping promises," *Fortune,* Special Issue, Winter/Autumn 1993, 32–34.

5. M. A. Hitt, R. D. Ireland, and R. E. Hoskisson, *Strategic Management: Competitiveness and Globalization.* (Minneapolis/St. Paul: West Publishing, 1995).

6. For example, see C. M. Fiol, "Managing culture as a competitive resource: An identity-based view of sustainable competitive advantage," *Journal of Management* 17 (1991): 191–211; J. B. Barney, "Organizational culture: Can it be a source of sustained competitive advantage?" *Academy of Management Review* 11 (1986): 656–665.

7. Barney, "Organizational culture."

8. T. E. Deal and A. A. Kennedy, *Corporate Cultures* (Reading, Mass.: Addison-Wesley, 1982).

9. For example, see D. R. Denison, *Corporate Culture and Organizational Effectiveness* (New York: Wiley, 1990); G. G. Gordon and N. DiTomaso, "Predicting corporate performance from organizational culture," *Journal of Management Studies* 32 (1992): 793–798;

J. P. Kotter and J. L. Heskett, *Corporate Culture and Performance* (New York: Free Press, 1992).

10. S. P. Robbins and M. Coulter, *Management* (Upper Saddle River, N.J.: Prentice Hall, 2003).

11. See, for example, Denison, *Corporate Culture and Organizational Effectiveness*; Gordon and DiTomaso, "Predicting corporate performance"; Kotter and Heskett, *Corporate Culture and Performance*.

12. J. A. Raelin, *Clash of Cultures* (Cambridge: Harvard Business School Press, 1986).

13. For a review of the effects of cultural diversity on organizational culture, see G. Hofstede, *Culture's Consequences: International Differences in Work-Related Values* (Beverly Hills, Calif.: Sage Publishers, 1980); W. E. Hopkins, *Ethical Dimensions of Diversity* (Thousand Oaks, Calif.: Sage Publishers, 1997).

14. A. Laurent, "The cultural diversity of western conceptions of management," *International Studies of Management and Organization* 13 (1983): 75–96.

15. W. Atkinson, "Managing the generation gap poses many challenges," *Hotel & Motel Management*, November 3, 2003, 72–74.

16. F. F. Brunel and M. R. Nelson, "Message order effects and gender differences in advertising persuasion," *Journal of Advertising Research*, September 2003, 330–341.

17. Ibid.

18. H. Cornelius, *The Gentle Revolution: Men and Women at Work: What Goes Wrong and How to Fix It* (Sydney: Simon & Schuster, 1998).

19. See, for example, A. Sharplin, *Strategic Management* (New York: McGraw-Hill, 1985).

20. J. Alexander and M. S. Wilson, "Leading across cultures: Five vital capabilities," in *The Organization of the Future*, ed. F. Hesselbein, M. Goldsmith, and R. Beckard (San Francisco: Jossey-Bass, 1997).

21. A. A. Thompson Jr. and A. J. Strickland III, *Strategic Management: Concepts and Cases* (Boston: McGraw-Hill, 1998).

22. These steps were suggested by P. Shrivastava, *Strategic Management: Concepts and Practices* (Cincinnati: South-Western Publishing, 1994).

Chapter 2: What Is Corporate Culture?

1. S. P. Robbins, *Essentials of Organizational Behavior* (Englewood Cliffs, N.J.: Prentice-Hall, 1984).

2. These descriptions were derived from the following sources: "The first global car colossus," *Business Week*, May 18, 1998, 42; "amazon.com: The wild world of e-commerce," *Business Week*, December 14, 1998, 110.

3. P. Hunsaker, *Training in Management Skills* (Upper Saddle River, N.J.: Prentice Hall, 2001).

4. Robbins, *Essentials of Organizational Behavior*.

5. E. H. Schein, *Organizational Culture and Leadership* (San Francisco: Jossey-Bass, 1985).

6. Information about this time line was found at http://www.hp.com/hpinfo.

7. H. M. Trice and J. M. Beyer, "Studying organizational cultures through rites and ceremonials," *Academy of Management Review* 9 (1984): 655.

8. A. M. Pettigrew, "On studying organizational cultures," *Administrative Science Quarterly*, December 1979, 576.

9. See B. Buell and R. D. Hof, "Hewlett Packard rethinks itself," *Business Week*, April 1, 1991, 76–79; C. Barnett, "On top at Hewlett Packard, John Young," *Visavis*, November 1991, 86.

10. HP News Release, Feb. 11, 2004. "HP Labs Founding Director Barney Oliver Inducted into National Inventors Hall of Fame." www.hp.com/hpinfo/newsroom/press.

11. This information was taken from the September 1993 issue of *Soap/Cosmetics/Chemical Specialties*.

12. P. Shrivastava, *Strategic Management: Concepts and Practices* (Cincinnati: South-Western Publishing, 1994).

13. E. H. Schein, "Organizational culture," *American Psychologist* 45 (1990): 109-119.

14. P. Gagliardi, *Symbols and Artifacts: Views of the Corporate Landscape* (New York: Aldine de Gruyter, 1990).

15. M. G. Pratt and A. Rafaeli, "Organizational dress as a symbol of multilayered social identities," *Academy of Management Journal* 40 (1997): 862–898.

16. See, for example, E. M. Eisenberg and P. Riley, "Organizational symbols and sensemaking," in *Handbook of Organizational Communication,* ed. G. M. Goldhaber and G. A. Barnett, 131–150 (Norwood, N.J.: Ablex, 1988); and D. A. Gioia, "Symbols, scripts, and sensemaking," in *The Thinking Organization,* ed. H. P. Sims, 49–74 (San Francisco: Jossey-Bass, 1986).

17. For example, see C. A. O'Reilly III, J. Chatman, and D. F. Caldwell, "People and organizational culture: A profile comparison approach to assessing person-organization fit," *Academy of Management Journal*, September 1991, 487–516; J. A. Chatman and K. A. Jehn, "Assessing the relationship between industry characteristics and organization culture: How different can you be?" *Academy of Management Journal*, June 1994, 522–553.

18. T. C. Deal and A. A. Kennedy, *Corporate Cultures: The Rites and Rituals of Corporate Life* (Reading, Mass.: Addison-Wesley, 1982).

19. This summary was adapted from *Organizational Culture,* by Carter McNamara, Ph.D., http://www.mapnp.org/library/org_thry/culture/culture.htm.

20. R. C. Ernest, "Corporate cultures and effective planning," *Personnel Administrator* 30 (1985): 52.

21. K. S. Cameron and R. E. Quinn, *Diagnosing and Changing Organizational Culture* (Reading, Mass.: Addison-Wesley, 1999).

22. E. A. Gerloff, *Organizational Theory and Design*. (New York: McGraw Hill, 1985).

23. For an in-depth discussion of climate and culture differences, see D. R. Denison, "What is the difference between organizational culture and organizational climate? A native's point of view on a decade of paradigm wars," *Academy of Management Review* 21 (1996): 619–654.

Chapter 3: Corporate Culture and Performance

1. T. L. Wheelen and J. D. Hunger, *Strategic Management* (Upper Saddle River, N.J.: Prentice Hall, 2000).

2. A. A. Thompson Jr. and A. J. Strickland III, *Strategic Management: Concepts and Cases* (Boston: McGraw-Hill, 2001).

3. Ibid.

4. Ibid.

5. Ibid.

6. Ibid.

7. This information was adapted from the following source: www.ideasformarketing.com.

8. See, for example, G. A. Steiner, J. B. Miner, and E. R. Gray, *Management Policy and Strategy: Text, Readings, and Cases* (New York: Macmillan, 1986).

9. J. N. Fry and J. P. Killing, *Strategic Analysis and Action* (Englewood Cliffs, N.J.: Prentice Hall, 1986).

10. G. Dessler, *Management: Principles and Practices for Tomorrow's Leaders* (Upper Saddle River, N.J.: Prentice Hall, 2004).

11. M. E. Porter, *Competitive Strategy: Techniques for Analyzing Industries and Competitors* (New York: Free Press, 1980).

12. L. Byars, *Strategic Management: Planning and Implementation, Concepts and Cases* (New York: Harper & Row, 1987).

13. P. M. Gutmann, "Strategies for growth," *California Management Review* 6 (1964): 31–36.

14. W. Skinner, "Getting physical: New strategic leverage from operations," *Journal of Business Strategy* 3 (1983): 75.

15. S. C. Myers, "Finance theory and financial strategy," *Interfaces* 14 (1984): 26–137.

16. L. Baird, I. Meshoulam, and G. DeGive, "Meshing human resource planning with strategic business planning: A model approach," *Personnel* 60 (1983): 17.

17. J. P. Kotter and J. L. Heskett, *Corporate Culture and Performance* (New York: Free Press, 1992), 7.

18. Thompson and Strickland, *Strategic Management.*

19. Ibid.

20. J. M. Higgins and J. W. Vincze, *Strategic Management Concepts* (Fort Worth, Tex.: Dryden, 1993).

21. Kotter and Heskett, *Corporate Culture and Performance.*

22. Ibid.

23. This example was reported by J. A. Pearce and R. B. Robinson Jr., *Strategic Management: Strategy Formulation and Implementation* (Homewood, Ill.: Richard D. Irwin, 1985).

24. G. Hofstede, *Culture's Consequences: International Differences in Work-Related Values* (Newbury Park, Calif.: Sage, 1980).

25. H. Schwartz and S. M. Davis, "Matching corporate culture and business strategy," *Organizational Dynamics,* Summer 1981, 30–48.

26. J. B. Barney, "Organizational culture: Can it be a source of sustained competitive advantage?" *Academy of Management Review* 2, no. 3 (1986): 656–665; J. A. Pearce and R. B. Robinson, *Formulation, Implementation, and Control of Competitive Strategy* (Homewood, Ill.: Irwin, 1994); Schwartz and Davis, "Matching corporate culture."

27. E. H. Schein, "The role of the founder in creating organizational culture," *Organizational Dynamics,* Summer 1983, 12–28.

28. J. G. March and H. A. Simon, *Organizations* (New York: Wiley, 1958).

29. B. Buchanan, "Building organizational commitment: The socialization of managers in work organizations," *Administrative Science Quarterly,* December 1974, 114–127; B. Buchanan, "To walk an extra mile: The whats, whens, and whys of organizational commitment," *Organizational Dynamics,* Spring 1975, 42–57.

30. R. M. Steers, *Organizational Effectiveness: A Behavioral View* (Santa Monica, Calif.: Goodyear, 1977); G. A. Steiner and J. B. Miner, *Management Policy and Strategy: Text, Readings, and Cases* (New York: Macmillan, 1977).

Chapter 4: Occupational Subcultures

1. E. Schein, "Culture: The missing concept in organization studies," *Administrative Science Quarterly* 41 (1996): 229–240.

2. S. A. Sackmann, "Culture and subcultures: An analysis of organizational knowledge," *Administrative Science Quarterly* 37 (1992): 140–161.

3. D. B. Drake, M. J. Koch, and N. A. Steckler, "Scientist, politician, and bureaucrat subcultures as barriers to information-sharing in government agencies." Proceedings of the 2003 National Conference on Digital Government Research, Boston, Mass.

4. *Monthly Labor Review*, U.S. Department of Labor, Bureau of Labor Statistics, November 1999; *Occupational Outlook Handbook*, U.S. Department of Labor, Bureau of Labor Statistics, 2004–2005 edition.

5. Ibid.

6. W. E. Hopkins and S. A. Hopkins, "Managing technology-oriented professionals," *Administrative Radiology*, 1988, 12: 22–25.

7. Ibid.

8. S. C. Certo, *Modern Management* (Upper Saddle River, N.J.: Prentice Hall, 2003).

9. G. J. Francis and G. Milbourn Jr., *Human Behavior in the Work Environment: A Managerial Perspective* (Santa Monica, Calif.: Goodyear, 1980); R. H. Hayes and S. C. Wheelwright, *Restoring Our Competitive Edge: Competing Through Manufacturing* (New York: John Wiley & Sons, 1984).

10. W. E. Hopkins and S. A. Hopkins, "Aligning cultures," *Administrative Radiology*, 1989, 12, 54–56.

11. F. Betz, *Managing Technology* (Englewood Cliffs, N.J.: Prentice Hall, 1987).

12. Hopkins and Hopkins, "Aligning cultures."

13. M. C. Paul, L. Waldera, K. Lahti, and A. Gans, *Culture Research Report* (Palo Alto, Calif.: InMomentum, 2000).

14. R. A. Buchholz, *Business Environment and Public Policy: Implications for Management and Strategy Formulation* (Englewood Cliffs, N.J.: Prentice-Hall, 1989).

15. Ibid.

16. W. Skinner, *Manufacturing: The Formidable Competitive Weapon* (New York: John Wiley & Sons, 1985).

17. Betz, *Managing Technology*.

18. A. Sharplin, *Strategic Management* (New York: McGraw-Hill, 1985).

19. W. Burke, ed., "Organization culture," *Organizational Dynamics* (special issue) 1983, 12, 5–80.

20. T. E. Deal and A. A. Kennedy, *Corporate Cultures: The Rites and Rituals of Corporate Life* (Reading, Mass.: Addison-Wesley, 1982).

21. Hayes and Wheelwright, *Restoring Our Competitive Edge*.

22. S. P. Robbins and M. Coulter, *Management* (Upper Saddle River, N.J.: Prentice Hall, 2002).

23. J. P. Workman, "Engineering's interactions with marketing groups in an engineering-driven organization," *IEEE Transactions on Engineering Management*, 1985, 42, 129–138.

Chapter 5: Ethnic and Racial Subcultures

1. For a full discussion of different cultural clusters, see D. A. De Cenzo, *Management* (Englewood Cliffs, N.J.: Prentice-Hall, 1988).

2. Sources of information for this section include: S. Steward, M. T. Cheung, and D. W. K. Yeung, "The South China economic community: The latest Asian newly industrialized economy emerges," *Columbia Journal of World Business* 27, no. 2 (1992): 30–37; D. J. Yang, S. Hutcheon, and J. Quek, "Is Asia breeding a whole pack of tigers?" *Business Week,* September 1990, 152–155; T. Andrew, "Samsung: South Korea marches to its own drummer," *Forbes,* May 16, 1988, 84–89.

3. Sources of information for this section include: I. Ratio and I. Rodgers, "A workshop on cultural differences," *AFS Orientation Handbook,* 1984, 4; N. Goodman, *Doing Business in Japan* (Randolph, N.J.: Global Dynamics, 1990); J. Orr, "Back in Tokyo," *CAE* 12, no. 3 (1993): 56; S. Sen, *Japan International Business Interact* (ABI, 1993).

4. Yuko, O. *Office Ladies and Salaried Men: Power, Gender, and Work in Japanese Companies.* Berkeley, University of California Press, 1998.

5. Sources of information for this section include: A. Singh, "Growth of urban centres, trade, commerce and industry in the Delhi sultanate," *Employment News* 18, no. 22 (1993): 1–2; B. M. Sinha, "India: Towards a social revolution," *Futures* 24, no. 9 (1992): 895–906; D. Lee and S. Tefft, "India is becoming the new Asian magnet for U.S. business," *Business Week,* May 1, 1989, 132; H. C. Jain, "Is there a coherent human resource management system in India?" *International Journal of Manpower* 12, no. 1 (1991): 10–17; J. P. Singh and G. Hofstede, "Managerial culture and work-related values in India: Reply and comment," *Organization Studies* 11, no. 1 (1990): 75–106.

6. Sources of information for this section include: S. Gutierrez, "Can you make it in Mexico?" *Financial Executive,* March-April 1993, 20–23; J.E.A. Gomez, "Mexican corporate culture," *Business Mexico* 3, no. 8 (1993): 8–9; D. O. Radebaugh, *International Business: Environments and Operations* (Reading, Mass.: Addison-Wesley, 1976); S. Thiederman, *Bridging Cultural Barriers for Corporate Success: How to Manage the Multicultural Work Force* (Los Angeles: Lexington Books, 1991).

7. Sources of information for this section include: P. P. Bose, "An economic iron curtain?" *McKinley Quarterly* 993, no. 1 (1993): 23–24; D. L. Hertz, "Developing management skills in Eastern Europe," *Journal of European Business* 3, no. 1 (1991): 60–61; R. F. Nicholls, "The neglected service industries of Eastern Europe: Some quantitative and qualitative aspects," *International Journal of Service Industry Management* 3, no. 3 (1992): 46–61; R. E. Axtell, *Do's and Taboos Around the World* (New York: John Wiley & Sons, 1985).

8. An acknowledgment is made here that the cultures of France and Great Britain are not necessarily representative of other cultures in Western Europe. However, their influence in this region has resulted in some similar cultural attributes among countries making up this cultural cluster.

9. Sources of information for this section include: H. E. Kramer, "Doing business in Germany and Australia: An Etic-Emic study of contrasts," *Management Decision* 30, no. 4

(1993): 52–56.; M. Malic, J. Rees, B. Johnstone, F. Chang, and R. Knowles, "Australia 1992: Paul primes the pump," *Far Eastern Economic Review* 155, no. 14 (1992): 33–45.; W. Kasper, "Advancing into the 21st century: Visions and challenges facing the downunder economy," *Australian Economic Review* 100 (1992): 51–54; H. Elton, "Still the luck country," *Australian Accountant* 62, no. 2 (1992): 32–35.

10. Sources of information for this section include: G. Hofstede, *Culture's Consequences: International Differences in Work-Related Values* (Beverly Hills, Calif.: Sage, 1980); S. E. Keefe, "Ethnic identity: The domain of perceptions of and attachment to ethnic groups and cultures," *Human Organizations* 51, no. 1 (1992): 35–43; R. C. Tung, "Managing cross-national and intra-national diversity," *Human Resource Management* 32, no. 4 (1993): 461–477; M. Piturro and S. S. Mahoney, "Managing diversity: The new multicultural workforce requires a simpatico style," *Executive Female,* May-June 1991, 45–48; A. Bennett, "American culture is often a puzzle for foreign managers in the U.S.," *Wall Street Journal,* February 12, 1986, 29.

11. Source: U.S. Census Bureau, 2004, "U.S. Interim Projections by Age, Sex, Race, and Hispanic Origin," www.census.gov.

12. B. Buchowicz, "Cultural transition and attitude change," *Journal of General Management* 15 (1990): 45–55; R. E. Petty and J. T. Cacioppo, *Attitudes and Persuasion: Classic and Contemporary Approaches* (Dubuque, Iowa: Wm. C. Brown, 1990).

13. R. Schauffler, "Children of immigrants," *National Forum* 74 (1994): 37–40.

14. A. Laurent, "The cultural diversity of western conceptions of management," *International Studies of Management and Organization* 13 (1983): 75–96.

15. J. Martin and C. Siehl, "Organizational culture and counter culture: An uneasy symbiosis," *Organizational Dynamics* 12, no. 2 (1983): 52–64; A. Sinclair, "Approaches to organizational culture and ethics," *Journal of Business Ethics* 12 (1993): 63–73; A. Wilkins and W. Ouchi, "Efficient cultures: Exploring the relationship between culture and organizational performance," *Administrative Science Quarterly* 28 (1983): 468–481.

Chapter 6: Gender and Generational Subcultures

1. Toossi, M. "Labor force projections to 2012: the graying of the U.S. workforce," *Monthly Labor Review,* February 2004, pp. 37–57.

2. Zeiger, D. "Women will dominate the 21st century workforce," *Business Plus,* October 27, 1992, pp. 6–7.

3. Ibid.

4. J. Millar and N. Jagger, *Women in ITEC Courses and Careers,* Report to Department for Education and Skills, Department for Trade and Industry and Women's Unit of the Cabinet Office, United Kingdom, University of Sussex, 2001.

5. L. L. Yaconi, "Cross-cultural role expectations in nine European country-units of a multinational enterprise," *Journal of Management Studies* 38 (2001): 1187–1215.

6. M. Linehan, "Women international managers: The European experience," *Cross Cultural Management* 8 (2001): 68–84.

7. B. Duffield, "Professional women in agriculture—do they have a future?" *Women in Management Review* 11 (1996): 20–27.

8. C. W. Ng, "Do women and men communicate differently at work? An empirical study in Hong Kong," *Women in Management Review* 13 (1998): 3–10.

9. A. M. W. Kubanek and M. Waller, *Confidence in Science: Interpersonal and Institutional Influences* (St. Anne de Bellevue: John Abbot College, 1996).

10. Linehan, "Women international managers"; M. Linehan and H. Scullion, "European female expatriate careers: Critical success factors," *Journal of European Industrial Training* 25 (2001): 392–418.

11. G. Sonnert and G. Holton, *Who Succeeds in Science? The Gender Dimension* (New Brunswick, N.J.: Rutgers University Press, 1995).

12. H. Etzkowitz, C. Kemelgor, M. Neuschatz, and B. Uzzi, "Barriers to women in academic science and engineering," in *Who Will Do Science? Educating the Next Generation*, ed. W. Pearson Jr. and I. Fletcher (Baltimore: Johns Hopkins University Press, 1994).

13. Linehan, "Women international managers."

14. H. Ibarra, "Homophily and differential returns: Sex differences in network structure and access in an advertising firm," *Administrative Science Quarterly* 37 (1992): 422–447.

15. For example, see S. G. Brush, "Women in science and engineering," *American Scientist* 79 (1991): 404–419; Etzkowitz et al., "Barriers to women"; S. V. Rosser, *Re-Engineering Female Friendly Science* (New York: Teachers College Press, 1991).

16. Sonnert and Holton, *Who Succeeds in Science?*

17. Duffield, "Professional women in agriculture."

18. J. H. Williams, *Psychology of Women: Behavior in a Biosocial Context* (New York: W. W. Norton, 1987).

19. L. M. Buckley, K. Sanders, M. Shih, S. Kallar, and C. Hampton, "Obstacles to promotion? Values of women faculty about career success and recognition," *Academic Medicine* 75 (2000): 283–288.

20. D. E. Giacomino and T. V. Eaton, "Personal values of accounting alumni: An empirical examination of differences by gender and age," *Journal of Managerial Issues* 15 (2003): 369–380.

21. The typology was developed by S. J. Musser and E. Orke, "Ethical value systems: A typology," *Journal of Applied Behavioral Science* 28 (1992): 348–362. The typology and the values survey are based on the work of M. Rokeach, *The Nature of Human Values* (New York: Free Press, 1973).

22. Source: U.S. Census Bureau, Census 2000 Summary File 1; http://www.census.gov/prod/2001pubs/c2kbr01-12.pdf.

23. Source: U.S. Bureau of Labor Statistics, February 2004.

24. Source: U.S. Census Bureau, Census 2000 Summary File 1; http://www.census.gov/prod/2001pubs/c2kbr01-12.pdf; Source: U.S. Bureau of Labor Statistics, February 2004.

25. Source: U.S. Census Bureau, Census 2000 Summary File 1; http://www.census.gov/prod/2001pubs/c2kbr01-12.pdf; Source: U.S. Bureau of Labor Statistics, February 2004.

26. Zinn, L., Power, C., Yang, D. J., Cuneo, A. Z., and Ross, D. "Move over boomers." *Business Week*, December 14: 74–82.

27. Source: www.gentrends.com

28. R. Zemke, C. Raines, and B. Filipczak, *Generations at Work: Managing the Clash of Veterans, Boomers, and Nexters in your Workplace*, (New York: Amacom, 2000).

29. D. King, "Defining a generation: Tips for uniting our multi-generational workforce." www.careerpmi.com/generations.htm

30. W. Atkinson, "Managing the generation gap poses many challenges," *Hotel & Motel Management*, November 3, 2003, 72–74.

31. R. Dubin, J. E. Champoux, and L. W. Porter, "Central life interests and organizational commitment of blue-collar and clerical workers," *Administrative Science Quarterly*, September 1975, 411–421; A. Kidron, "Work values and organizational commitment," *Academy of Management Journal*, June 1978, 239–247.

32. B. W. Shimko, "Pre-hire assessment of the new work force: Finding wheat (and work ethic) among the chaff," *Business Horizons*, May-June 1992, 60–65.

33. J. Sheedy, "The work force of tomorrow," *Harvard Business Review*, September-October 1990, 234–235.

34. Giacomino and Eaton, "Personal values of accounting alumni."

Chapter 7: Diagnosing Corporate Culture Alignment

1. S. P. Robbins, *Essentials of Organizational Behavior* (Englewood Cliffs, N.J.: Prentice-Hall, 1984).

2. The following Web sites represent a sample of organizations that provide survey-developing services for diagnosing corporate culture:

http://www.busreslab.com/culture-surveys.htm

http://www.stormindex.com/surveys.html

http://www.ownershipassociates.com/surveys.htm

3. For further information on data analysis techniques, we refer you to any basic business statistics textbook.

4. T. E. Deal and A. A. Kennedy, *Corporate Cultures* (Reading, Mass.: Addison-Wesley, 1982).

5. Ibid.

6. These symptoms were set forth by P. Bate, "The impact of organizational culture on approaches to organizational problem-solving," *Organizational Studies* 1 (1984): 49–58.

7. These symptoms were set forth by L. W. Rue and P. G. Holland, *Strategic Management: Concepts and Experiences* (New York: McGraw-Hill, 1986).

8. These diagnostic activities were suggested by Deal and Kennedy, *Corporate Cultures.*

9. These points were suggested by C. Selltiz, M. Jahoda, M. Deutsch, and S. Cook, *Research Methods in Social Relations* (New York: Holt, Rinehart and Winston, 1959).

10. Ibid.

11. Paul Barribeau, Bonnie Butler, Jeff Corney, Megan Doney, Jennifer Gault, Jane Gordon, Randy Fetzer, Allyson Klein, Cathy Ackerson Rogers, Irene F. Stein, Carroll Steiner, Heather Urschel, Theresa Waggoner, and Mike Palmquist (2005). Survey research. Writing@CSU, Colorado State University, Department of English. Retrieved February 15, 2005 from http://writing.colostate.edu/references/research/survey/.

12. Ibid.

13. Selltiz et al., *Research Methods in Social Relations.*

14. Ibid.

15. Ibid.

16. Ibid.

Chapter 8: Assessing Strategic Vision

1. L. Larwood, C. M. Falbe, M. P. Kriger, and P. Miesing, "Structure and meaning of organizational vision," *Academy of Management Journal* 39, no. 3 (1995): 740–769.

2. P. Senge, *The Fifth Discipline* (New York: Currency-Doubleday, 1990).

3. N. M. Tichy and S. Sherman, *Control Your Destiny or Someone Else Will* (New York: Currency-Doubleday, 1993).

4. M. Tichy and R. Charan, "Speed, simplicity, self-confidence: An interview with Jack Welch," *Harvard Business Review*, September-October, 1989, 112–120.

5. "Gerstner's non-vision for IBM raises a management issue," *Wall Street Journal*, July 29, 1993, B1.

6. Ibid.

7. Senge, *The Fifth Discipline.*

8. J. R. Lucas, "Anatomy of a vision statement," *Management Review*, February 1998, 22–26.

9. Ibid.

10. Senge, *The Fifth Discipline.*

11. J. Collins and J. I. Poras, "Building your company's vision," *Harvard Business Review,* September-October 1996, 65–77.

12. J. Collins, *Good to Great* (New York: Harper-Collins, 2001).

13. Senge, *The Fifth Discipline.*

14. B. Nanus, *Visionary Leadership* (San Francisco: Jossey-Bass, 1992).

15. Collins and Poras, "Building your company's vision."

16. I. Wilson, "Realizing the power of strategic vision," *Long Range Planning* 25, no. 2 (1992): 18–28.

17. Ibid.

Chapter 9: Confirming Corporate Values

1. J. Collins and J. I. Poras, *Built to Last: Successful Habits of Visionary Companies* (New York: Random House Business Books, 1994).

2. Ibid.

3. "How a values-based culture pays off," *HRFocus* 79, no. 10 (2002): 1–3.

4. R. M. Kanter, *Men and Women of the Corporation* (New York: Basic Books, 1993).

5. W. Bennis, "'Owed' to Rosabeth Moss Kanter: Impact on management practice," *Academy of Management Executive* 18, no. 2 (2004): 106–107.

6. A. Mehra and M. Kilduff, "At the margins: A distinctive approach to the social identity and social networks of women and racial minorities," *Academy of Management Review* 41, no. 4 (1998): 441–453.

7. H. Ibarra, "Men and women of the corporation and the change masters: Practical theories for changing times," *Academy of Management Executive* 18, no. 2 (2004): 108–111.

8. T. E. Deal and A. A. Kennedy, *Corporate Culture: The Rites and Rituals of Corporate Life* (Reading, Mass.: Addison-Wesley, 1982).

9. J. P. Kotter and J. L. Heskett, *Corporate Culture and Performance* (New York: Free Press, 1992).

10. E. H. Schein, *Organizational Culture and Leadership* (San Francisco: Jossey-Bass, 1993).

11. Kotter and Heskett, *Corporate Culture and Performance.*

12. P. M. Lencioni, "Make your values mean something," *Harvard Business Review,* July 2002, 113–117.

13. J. Thornbury, "Creating a living culture: The challenges for business leaders," *Corporate Governance* 3, no. 2 (2003): 68–79.

14. Lencioni, "Make your values mean something."

15. J. Collins and J. I. Poras, "Building your company's vision," *Harvard Business Review,* September-October 1996, 65–77.

16. Lencioni, "Make your values mean something."

17. N. M. Tichy and S. Sherman, *Control Your Destiny or Someone Else Will* (New York: Currency-Doubleday, 1993).

Chapter 10: Communicating Vision and Values

1. G. G. Gordon, "The relationship of corporate culture to industry sector and corporate performance," in *Gaining Control of the Corporate Culture*, ed. R. H. Kilmann, M. J. Saxton, R. Serpa, and Associates (San Francisco: Jossey-Bass, 1985), 123; T. Kono, "Corporate culture and long-range planning," *Long Range Planning*, August 1990, 9–19.

2. M. DePree, *Leadership Is an Art* (New York: Dell, 1989), 82, 108.

3. J. P. Kotter and J. L. Heskett, *Corporate Culture and Performance* (New York: Free Press, 1992).

4. S. Ober, *Contemporary Business Communication* (Boston: Houghton-Mifflin, 2001), 17.

5. J. A. Conger, "Inspiring others: The language of leadership," *Academy of Management Executive* 5, no. 1 (1991): 31–45.

6. Ibid.

7. Ibid.

8. F. Westley and H. Mintzberg, "Profiles of strategic visions Levesque and Iacocca," in *Charismatic Leadership: The Elusive Factor in Organizational Effectiveness,* ed. J. A. Conger and R. N. Kanungo (San Francisco: Jossey-Bass, 1988), 161–212.

9. Conger, "Inspiring others."

10. M. M. Osborn and D. Ehninger, "The metaphor in public address," *Speech Monograph* 29 (1962), 228.

11. E. Borgida and R. E. Nisbett, "The differential impact of abstract vs. concrete information on decisions," *Journal of Applied Technology* 7, no. 3 (1977): 258–271.

12. This excerpt of Dr. King's speech is quoted in Conger, "Inspiring others." 42.

13. A. R. Willner, *The Spellbinders* (New Haven: Yale University Press, 1984), 164.

14. Conger, "Inspiring others."

15. Ibid.

16. Ibid. 40.

17. S. Ober, *Contemporary Business Communication.*

18. Ibid.

19. Here, we are specifically referring to African Americans, Anglo-Americans, Asian Americans, Hispanic Americans, and Native Americans.

20. S. A. Hopkins, W. E. Hopkins, and B. Thornton, "High-tech success in low-tech environments: Culture and human resource contingencies." *SAM Advanced Management Journal,* 67: 14-22, 2002.

21. S. Ober, *Contemporary Business Communication.*

22. J. Coates, *Women, Men, and Language* (New York: Longman, 2001); D. Tannen, *You Just Don't Understand* (New York: Ballantine, 1990); J. Gray, *Men Are from Mars, Women Are from Venus* (New York: HarperCollins, 1992); P. Hathaway, *Giving and Receiving Feedback,* rev. ed. (Menlo Park, Calif.: Crisp, 1998); D. Tannen, *Talking from 9 to 5* (New York: William Morrow, 1994).

23. Ober, S. *Contemporary Business Communication.* (Boston: Houghton Mifflin Company, 2001).

Chapter 11: Building Commitment to Vision and Values

1. Hesselbein et al., *The Organization of the Future.*

2. S. C. Harper, "The challenges facing CEOs: Past, present, and future," *Academy of Management Executive* 6, no. 3 (1992): 7–19.

3. F. Hesselbein, M. Goldsmith, and R. Beckhard, *The Organization of the Future* (San Francisco: Jossey-Bass, 1997).

4. T. E. Deal and A. A. Kennedy, *Corporate Culture: The Rites and Rituals of Corporate Life* (Reading, Mass.: Addison-Wesley, 1982).

5. Hesselbein et al., *The Organization of the Future.*

6. S. P. Robbins, *The Truth About Managing People* (New York: Prentice-Hall, 2003).

7. Deal and Kennedy, *Corporate Culture.*

8. J. Collins and J. I. Poras, "Building your company's vision," *Harvard Business Review,* September-October 1996, 65–77.

9. Ibid.

10. Deal and Kennedy, *Corporate Culture.*

11. Robbins, *The Truth About Managing People.*

12. Collins and Poras, "Building your company's vision."

13. Kotter and Heskett, *Corporate Culture and Performance.*

Chapter 12: Maintaining Subculture Alignment

1. Robert H. Kent, *Installing Change: An Executive Guide for Implementing and Maintaining Organizational Change* (Winnipeg: Pragma Press, 2001).

2. R. Jacobson, K. Setterholm, and J. Vollum, *Leading for a Change: How to Master the Five Challenges Faced by Every Leader* (Boston: Butterworth Heinemann, 2000).

3. E. A. Gerloff, *Organizational Theory and Design* (New York: McGraw Hill, 1985).

4. T. C. Deal and A. A. Kennedy, *Corporate Cultures: The Rites and Rituals of Corporate Life* (Reading, Mass.: Addison-Wesley, 1982).

5. These were suggested by W. G. Bennis, K. D. Benne, and R. Chin, *The Planning of Change* (New York: Holt, Rinehart and Winston, 1969); and A. Newell and H. A. Simon, *Human Problem Solving* (Englewood Cliffs, N.J.: Prentice-Hall, 1972).

6. N. L. Frigon, Sr. and H. K. Jackson, Jr., *The Leader: Developing the Skills and Personal Qualities You Need to Lead Effectively* (New York: Amacom, 1996).

7. L. P. White and K. C. Wooten, "Ethical dilemmas in various stages of organizational development," *Academy of Management Review* 8 (1983): 690–697.

Index